50 CUTE CHRISTMAS DRAWINGS

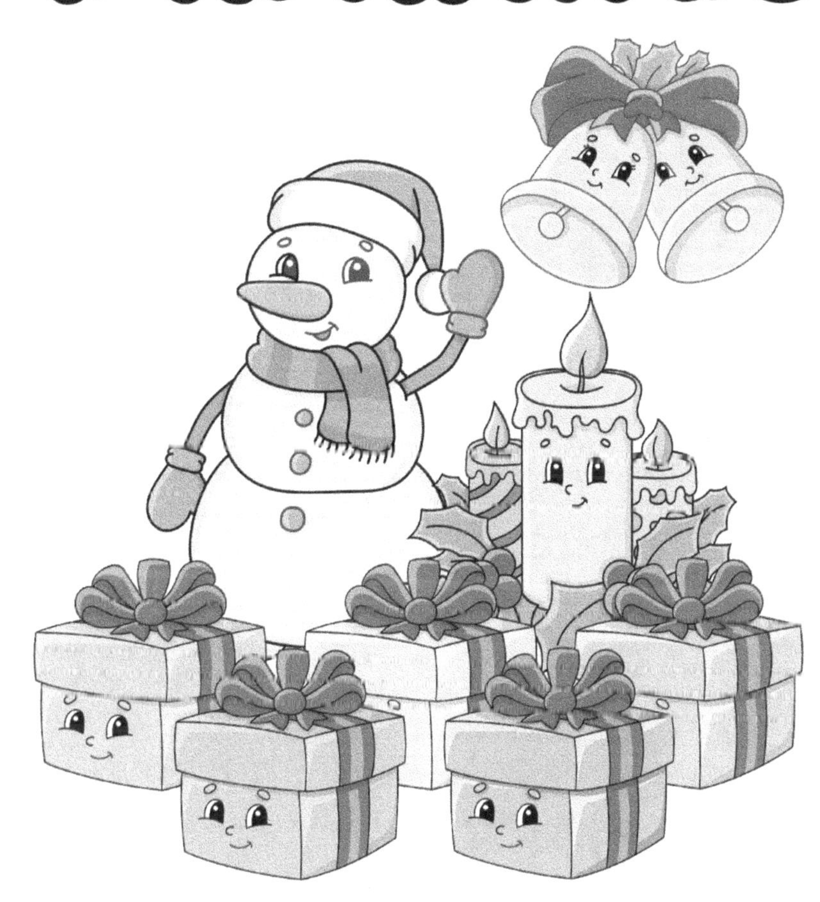

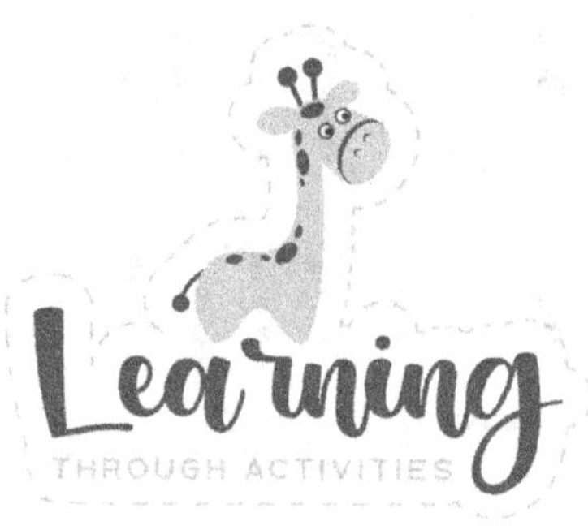

SPECIAL BONUS!

Want These 2 Books For FREE?

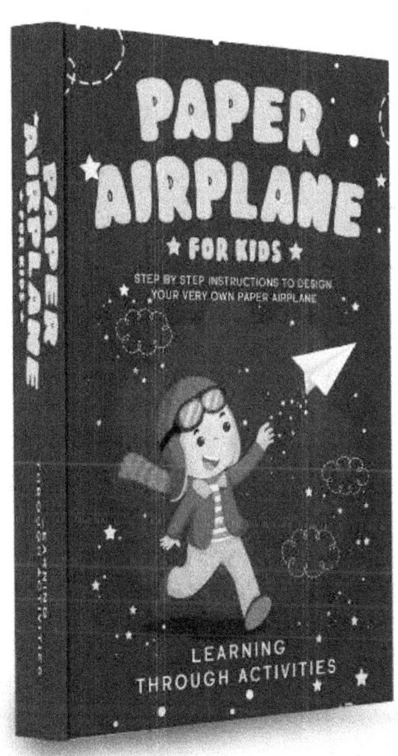

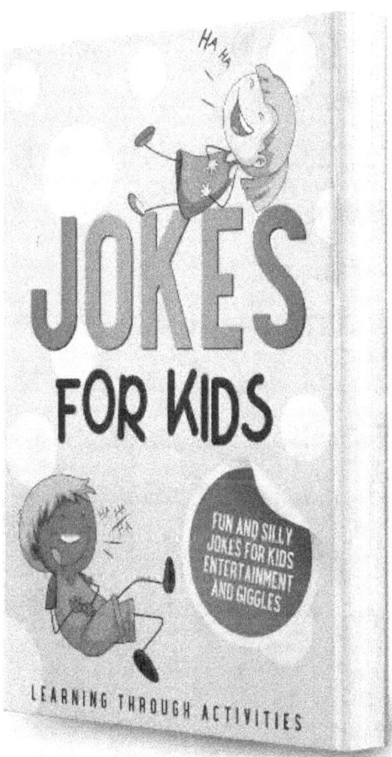

Get **FREE**, unlimited access to these and all of our new kids books by joining our community!

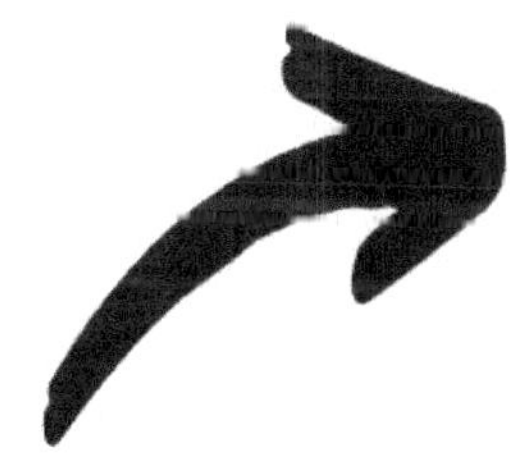

Scan W/ Your Camera To Join!

CONTENTS

INTRODUCTION

WELCOME TO 'HOW TO DRAW FOR KIDS – CHRISTMAS EDITION' THIS BOOK IS FULL OF EVERYTHING TO DO WITH CHRISTMAS! YOU'LL BE AN ARTIST BEFORE YOU KNOW IT!

EACH CHRISTMAS DRAWING HAS EASY TO FOLLOW INSTRUCTIONS THAT WILL STEP-BY-STEP HAVE YOU DRAWING THEM LIKE A PRO!

NOT ONLY WILL YOU LEARN HOW TO DRAW ALL OF THESE AMAZINGLY FUN OBJECTS AND CHARACTERS, YOU WILL ALSO LEARN HOW THEY LIVE, AND WHAT EACH LOVES MOST ABOUT CHRISTMAS!

PLEASE DON'T WORRY IF YOUR DRAWINGS TURN OUT A LITTLE DIFFERENT FROM THE ONES IN THE PICTURES, WE ALL HAVE OUR UNIQUE STYLE, AND ALSO, PRACTICE MAKES PERFECT!

GENERALLY, IT'S BEST TO START WITH A PENCIL WHILE YOU ARE GETTING THE HANG OF IT, SO LITTLE MISTAKES CAN BE EASILY ERASED. THEN MOVE ONTO PENS, COLORED, SPARKLY, WHATEVER YOU LIKE.

HAVE FUN!

EYES

NORMAL

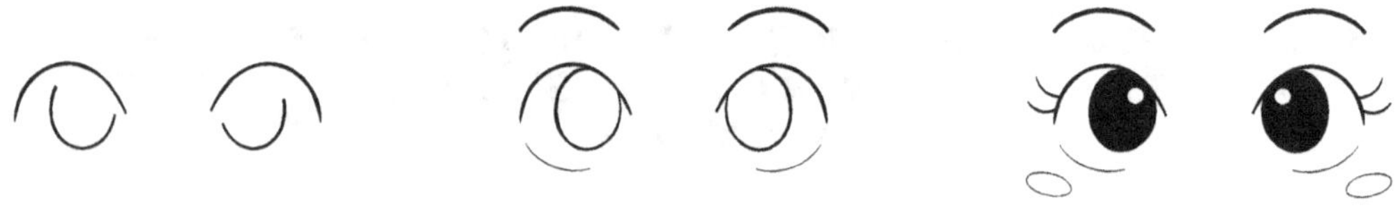

HAPPY

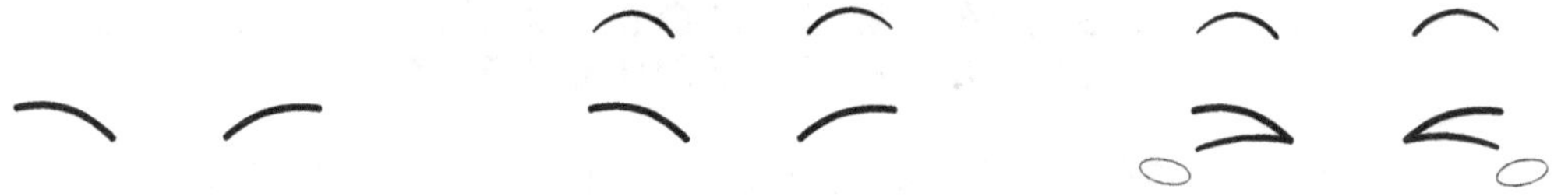

WINK

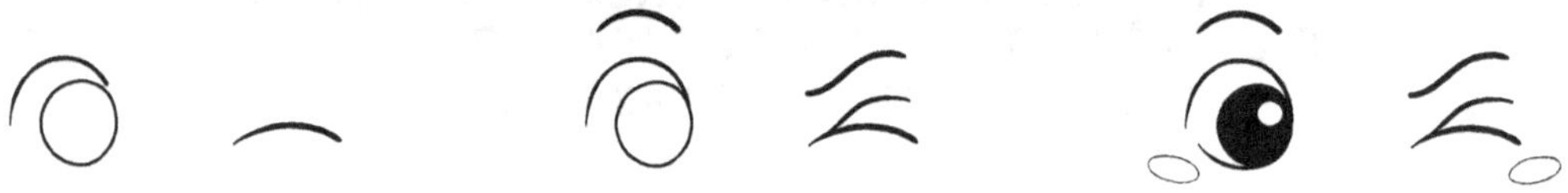

SPY / SMART

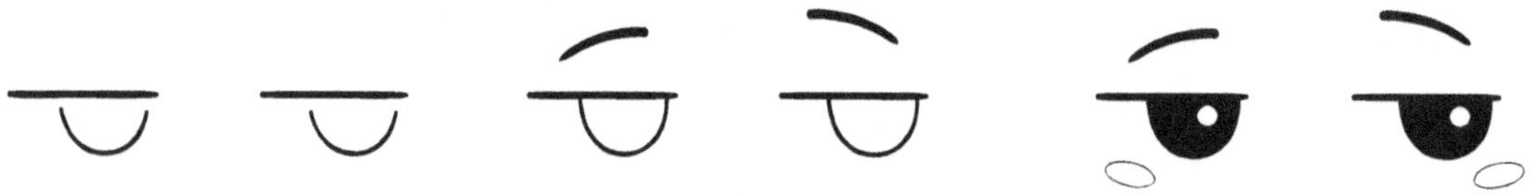

SLEEPY / SHY

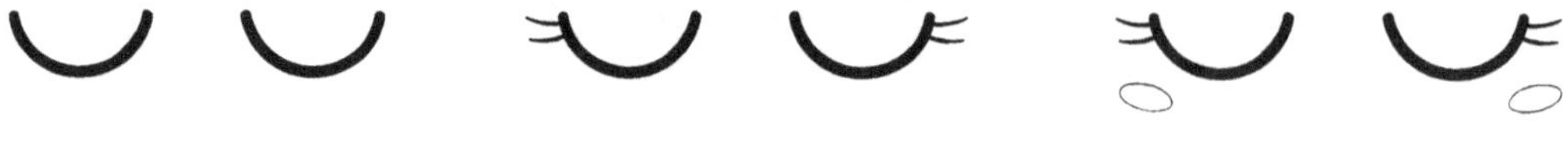

ASTONISHED

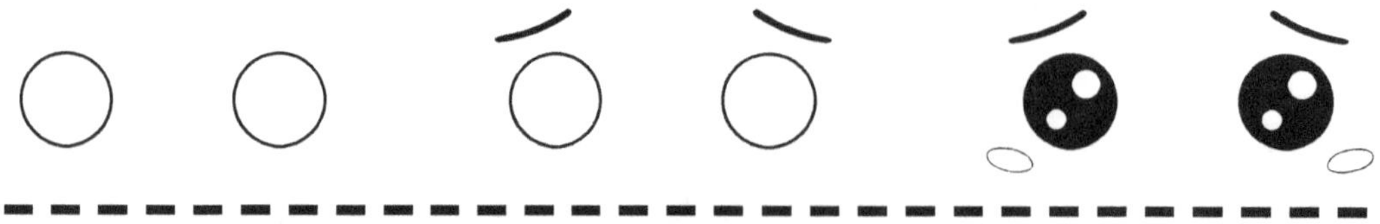

SWEETY STOCKING

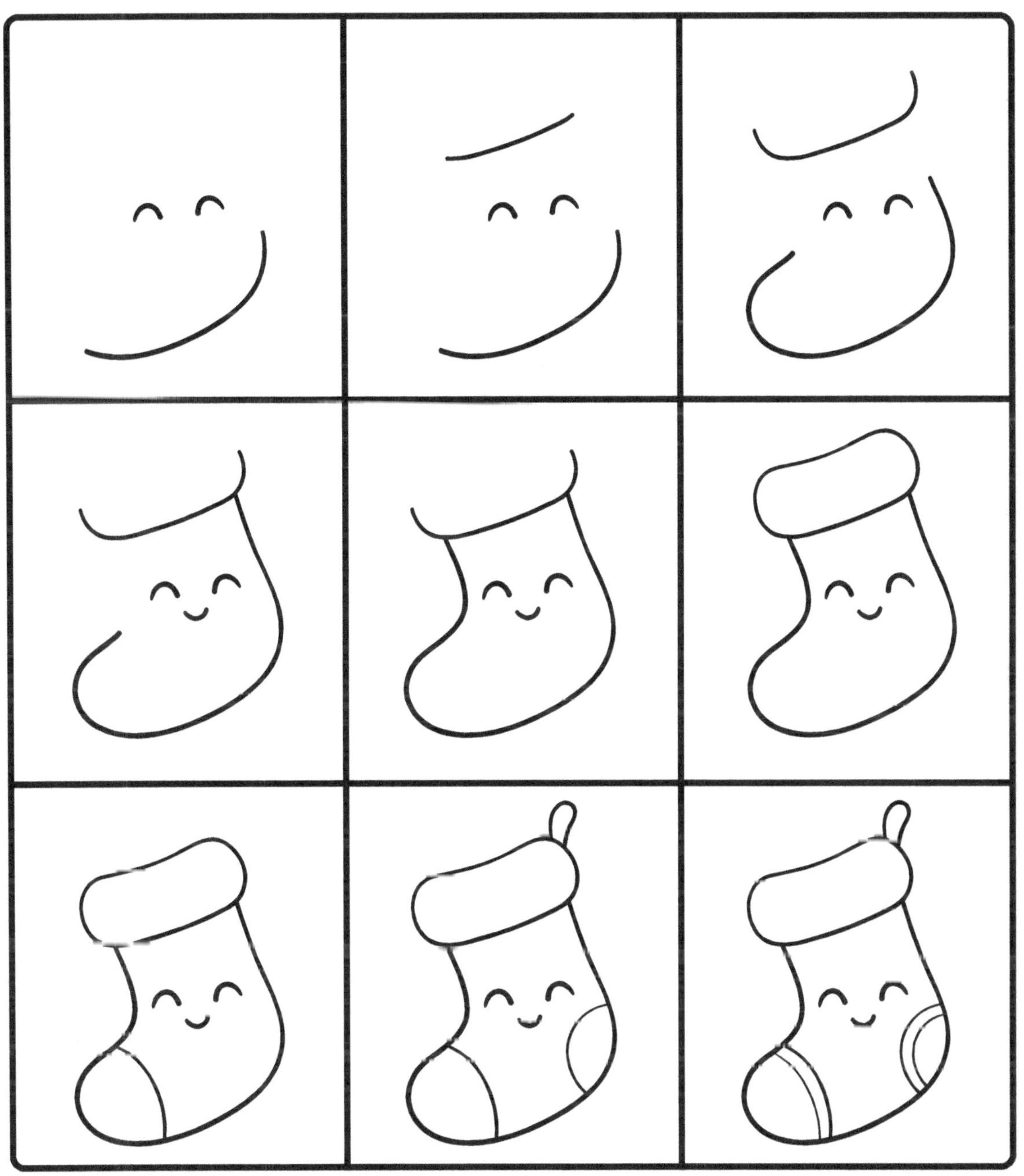

SIR FIR

LIVES:
TOWERING IN THE ENTRANCE OF A BIG DEPARTMENT STORE.

LOVES MOST ABOUT CHRISTMAS:
WATCHING ALL THE SHOPPERS BUSTLE IN AND OUT OF THE STORE WITH COLORFUL BAGS OF GIFTS.

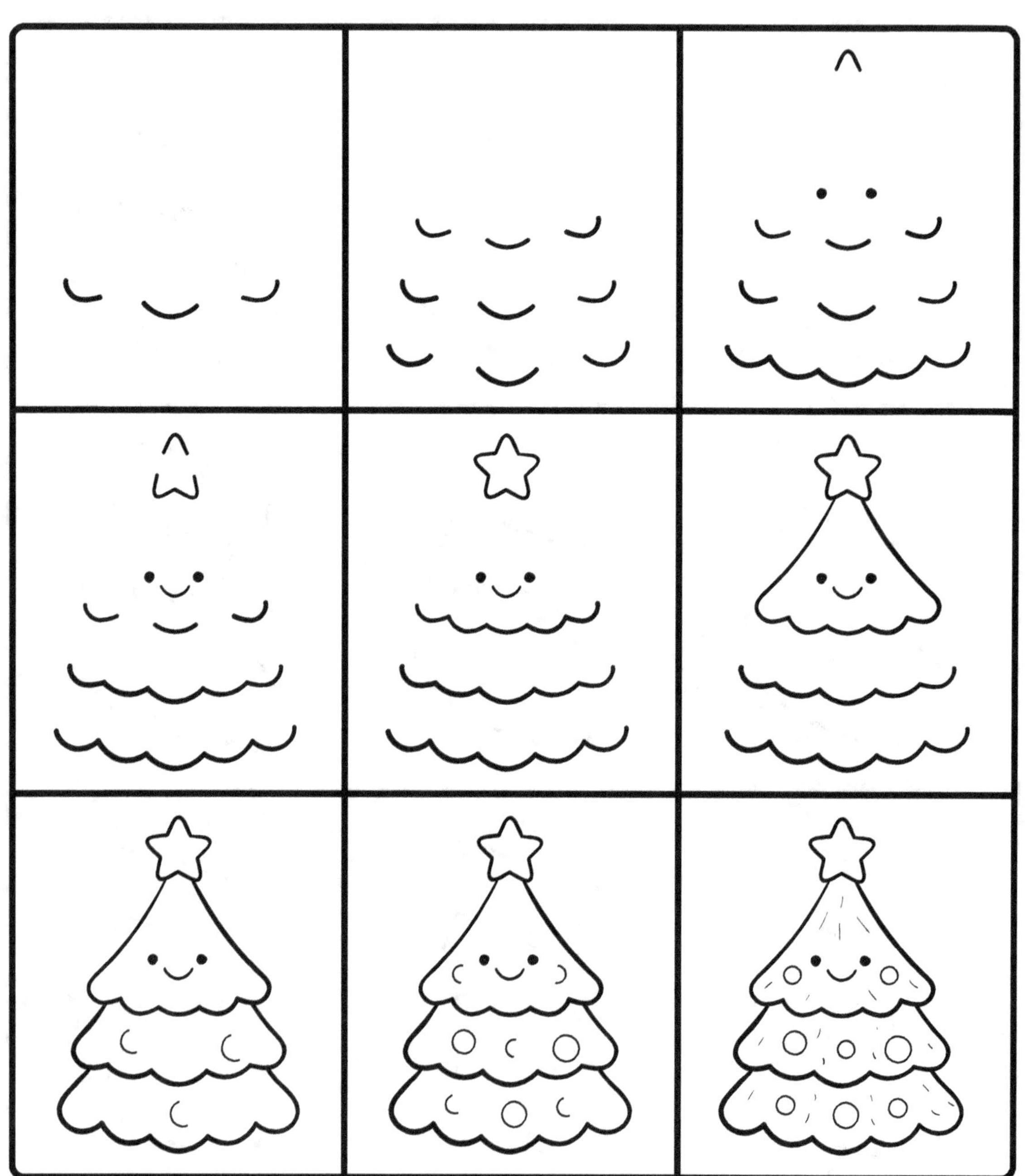

GINGY

ON A BAKING TRAY, STILL WARM FROM THE OVEN.

BEING DECORATED WITH ICING BY EXCITED CHILDREN.

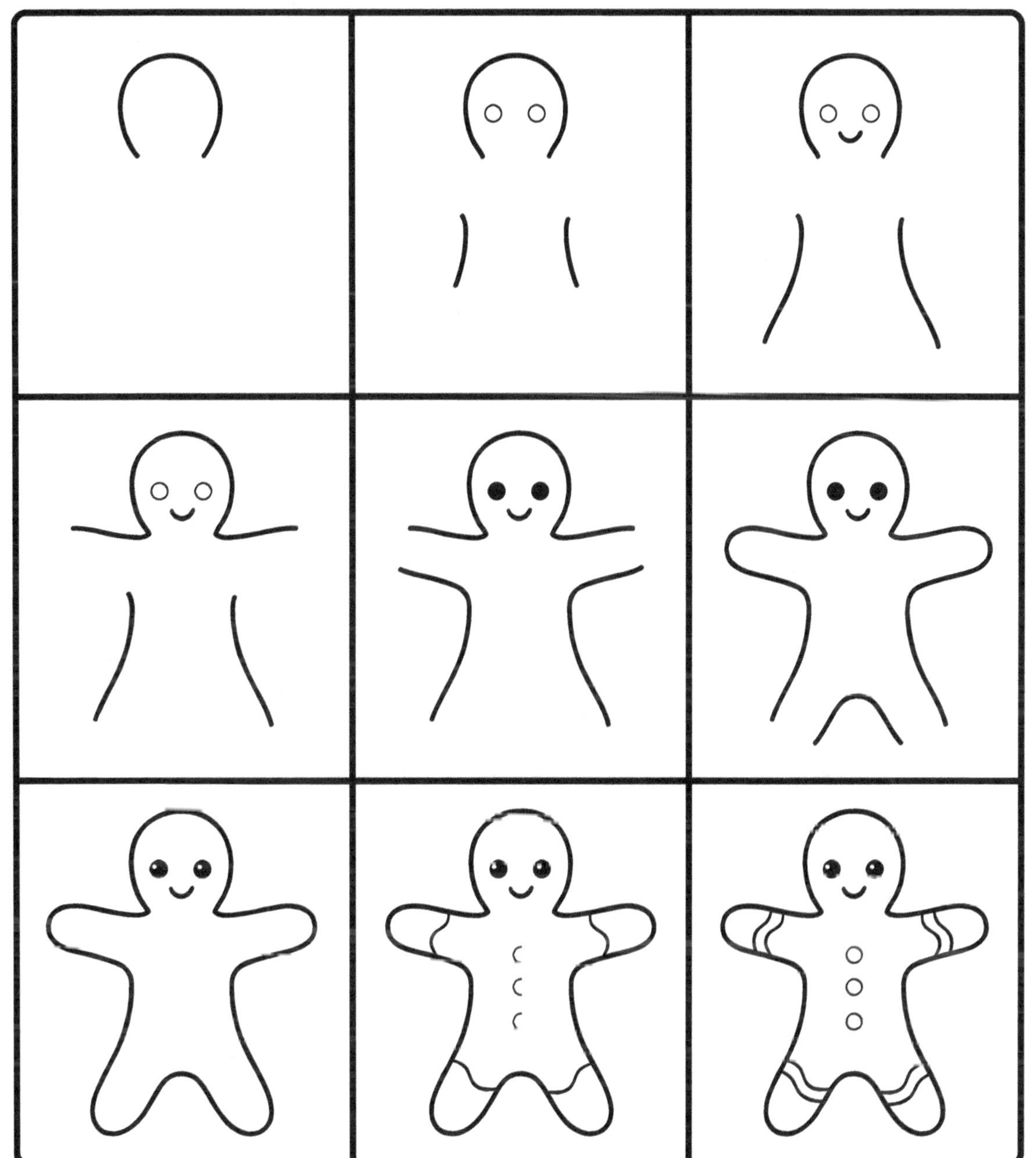

MISTLETWO

LIVES:
ON A TREE, ON THE EDGES OF A FOREST IN GREECE.

LOVES MOST ABOUT CHRISTMAS:
BEING PICKED OFF THE TREE, KNOWING IT WILL BE SOON HUNG UP FOR PEOPLE TO ADMIRE FROM UNDERNEATH.

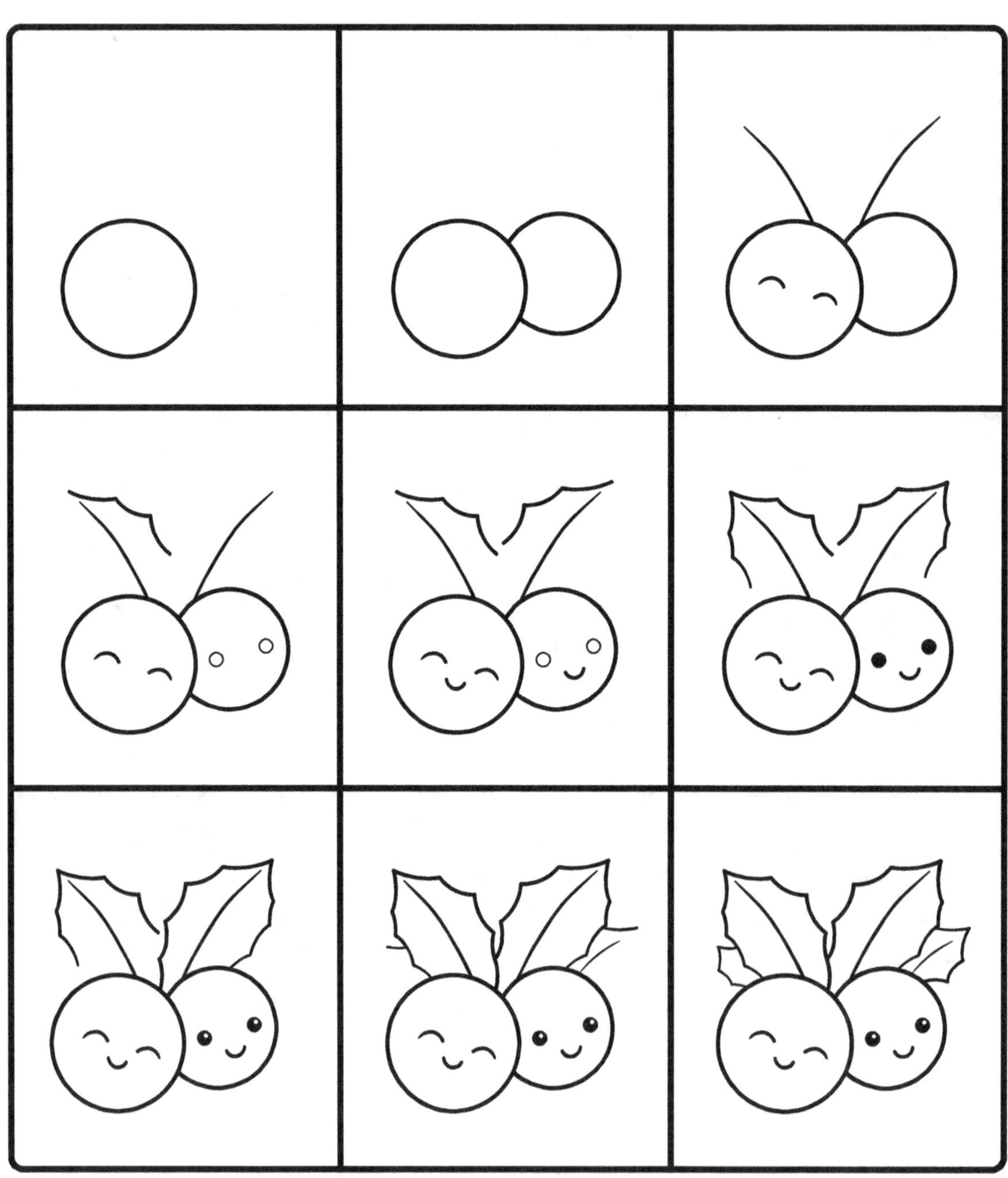

SANTA'S SLEIGH

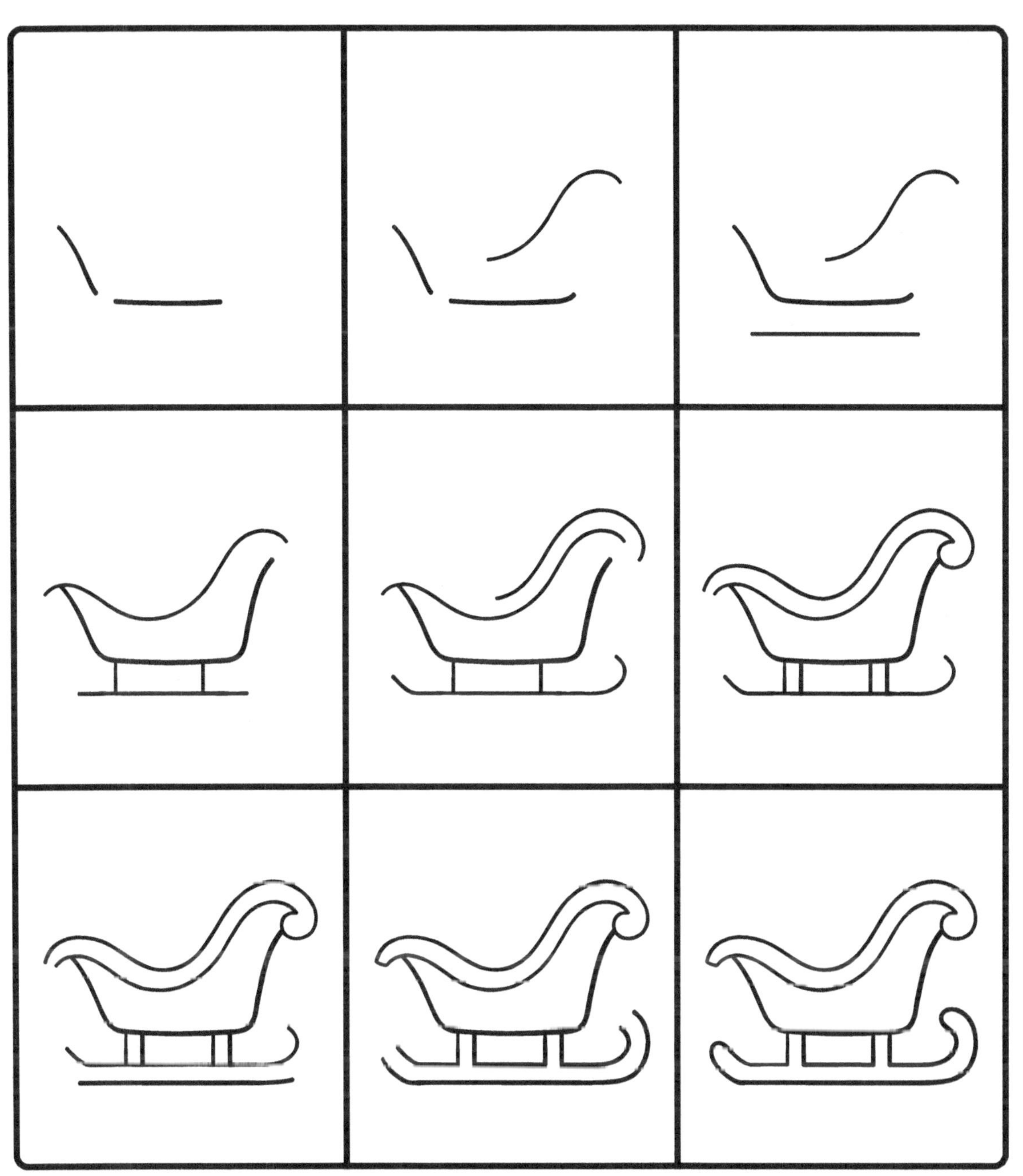

SMITTEN MITTEN

ON SANTA'S HAND!

HOLDING ONTO THE REINS OF THE
REINDEERS AS THEY FLY UNDER
TWINKLING STARS ON CHRISTMAS EVE.

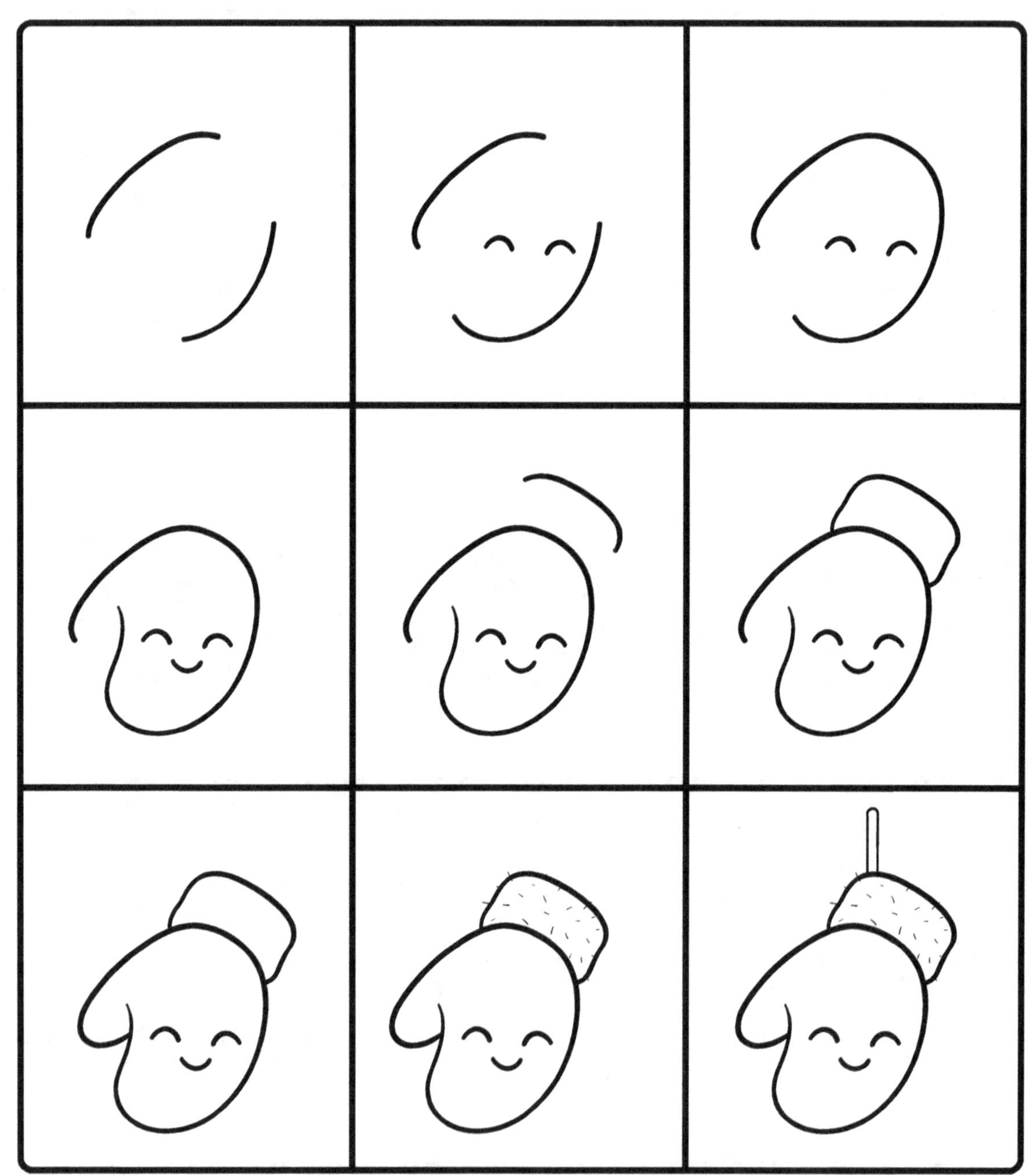

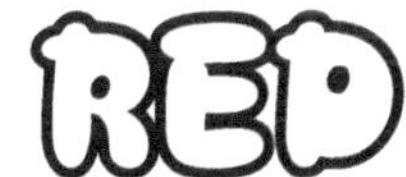
RED

LIVES:
ON SANTA'S HEAD!

LOVES MOST ABOUT CHRISTMAS:
SLIDING DOWN ALL OF THE CHIMNEYS
WITH SANTA. WHOOSH!

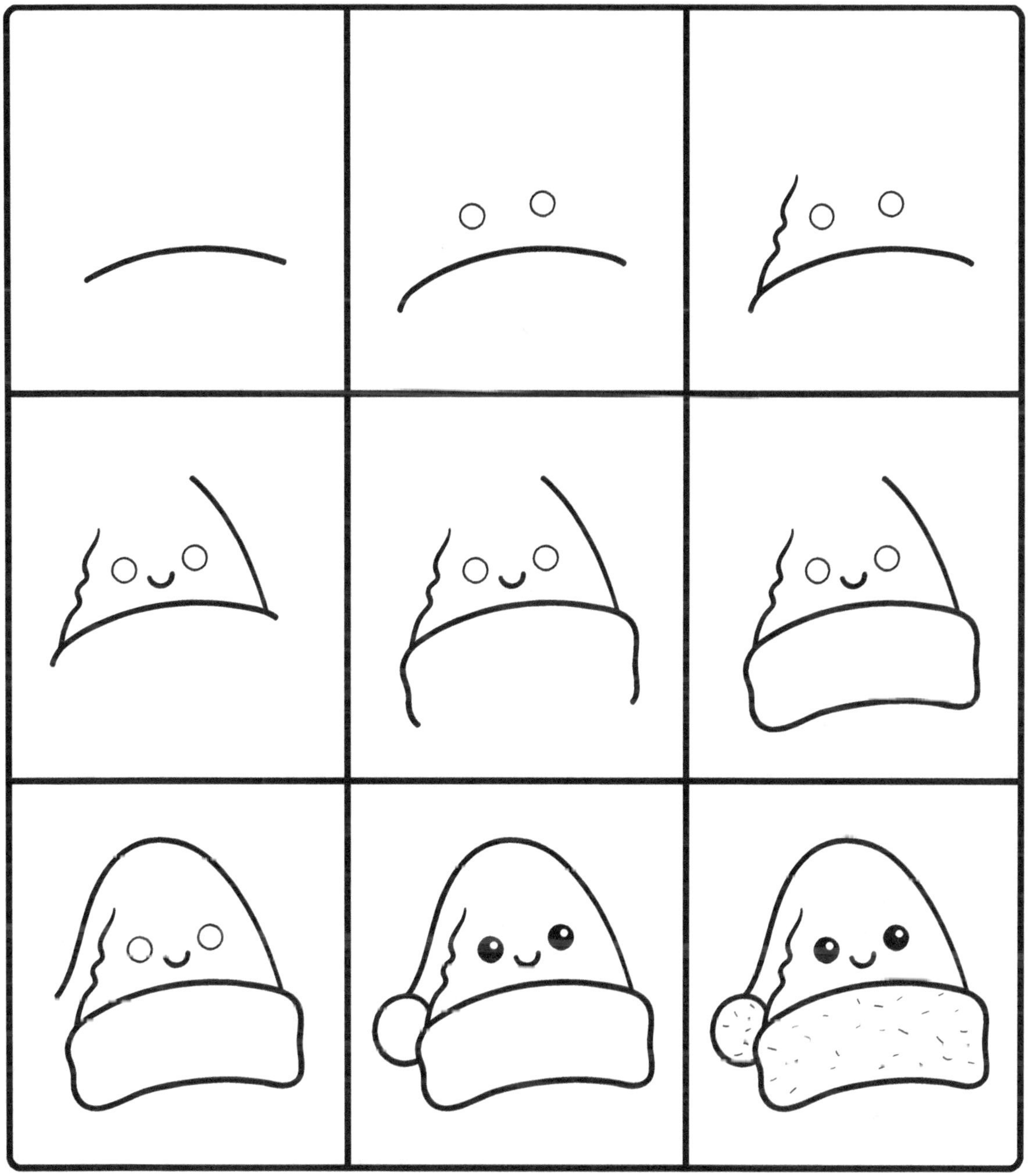

PREZZIE

LIVES:
UNDER THE TREE, WAITING EXCITEDLY TO BE OPENED.

LOVES MOST ABOUT CHRISTMAS:
CROSSING OFF THE DAYS COUNTING DOWN TO BEING OPENED.

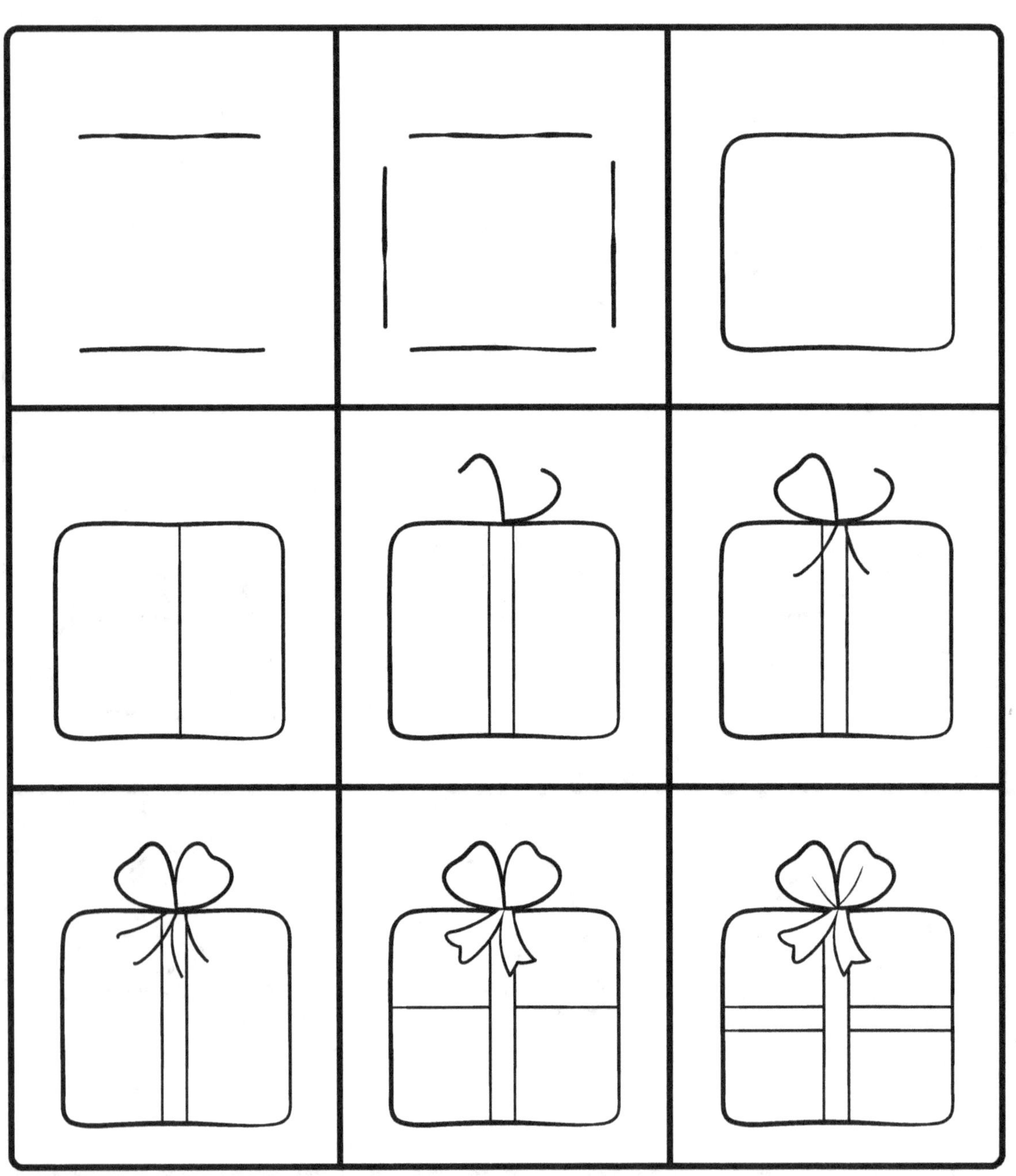

STAR-TIP

RIGHT ON TOP OF THE CHRISTMAS TREE.

FEELING SUPER SPECIAL - BEING THE
LAST TO BE PUT ON THE TREE BY A CHILD
HELP UP HIGH.

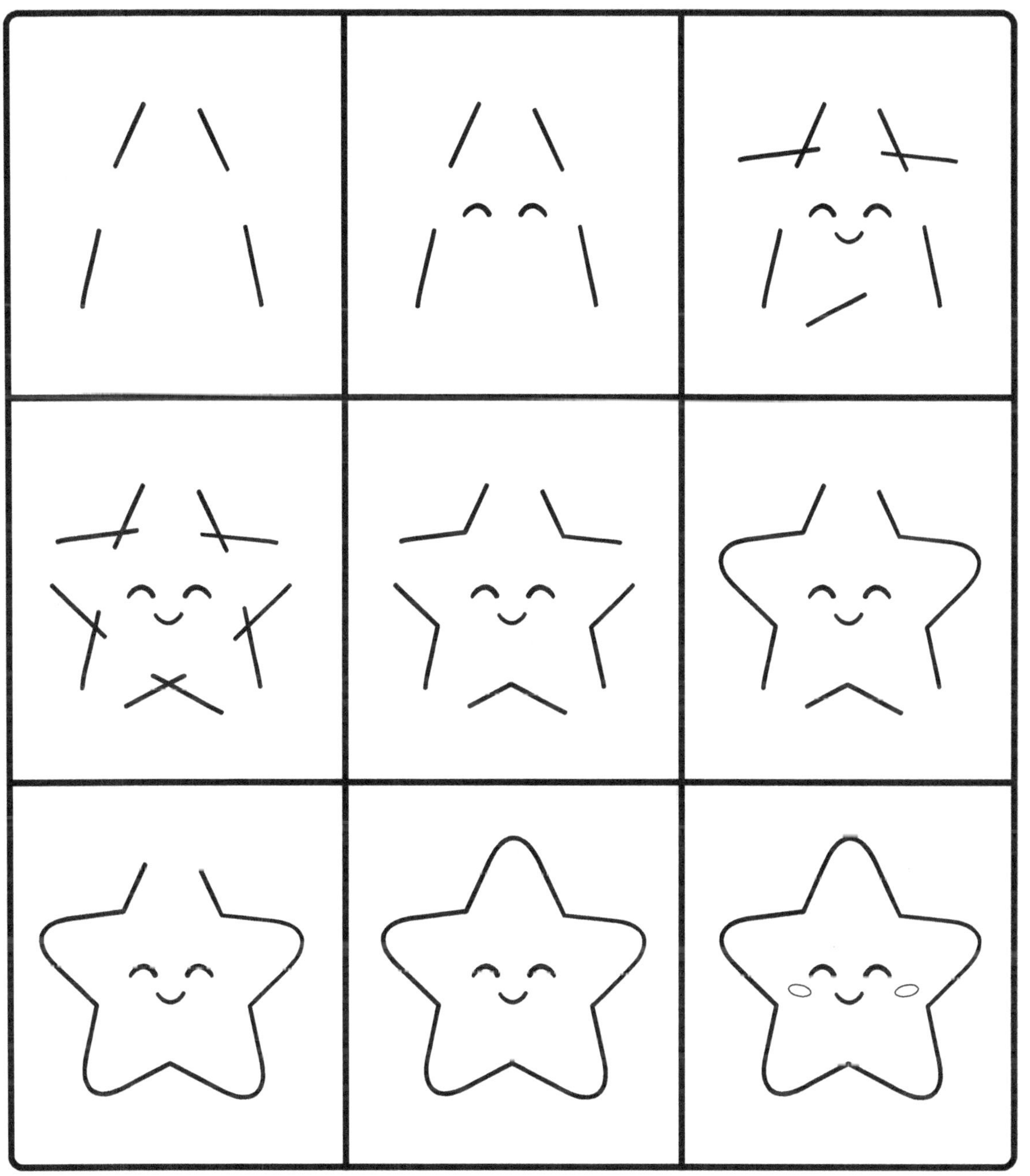

ON THE BOTTOM BRANCH OF THE TREE, RIGHT ABOVE THE PILED-UP GIFTS.

THE MOMENT WHEN HE IS TAKEN OUT OF THE BOX AND PLACED ONTO THE TREE, ALWAYS IN A DIFFERENT SPOT EACH YEAR.

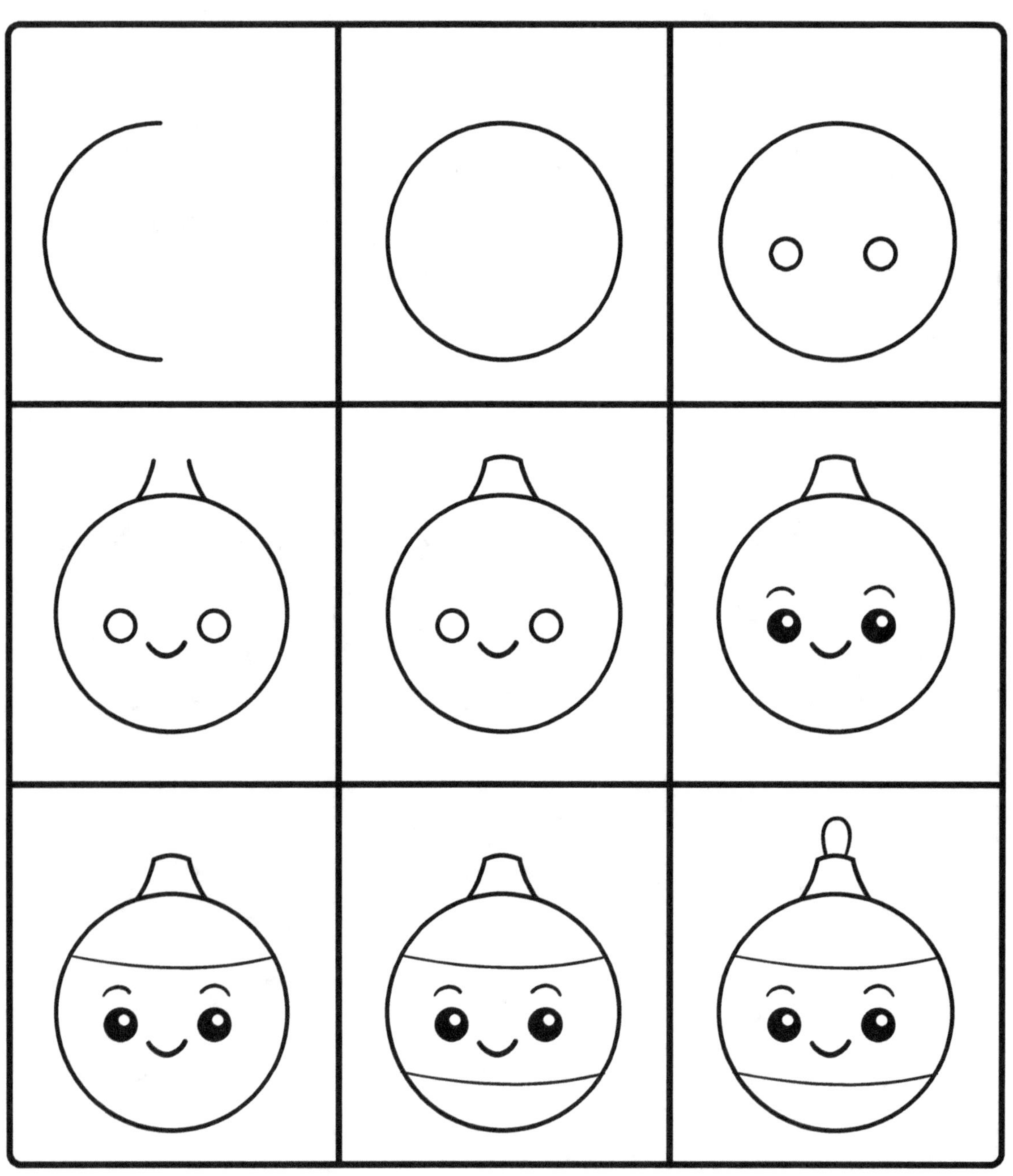

BELLE

LIVES:
HANGING ON A GARLAND UNDER THE MANTLEPIECE.

LOVES MOST ABOUT CHRISTMAS:
WHEN KIDDIES TINKLE HER AS THEY PASS BY. RING, RING RING!

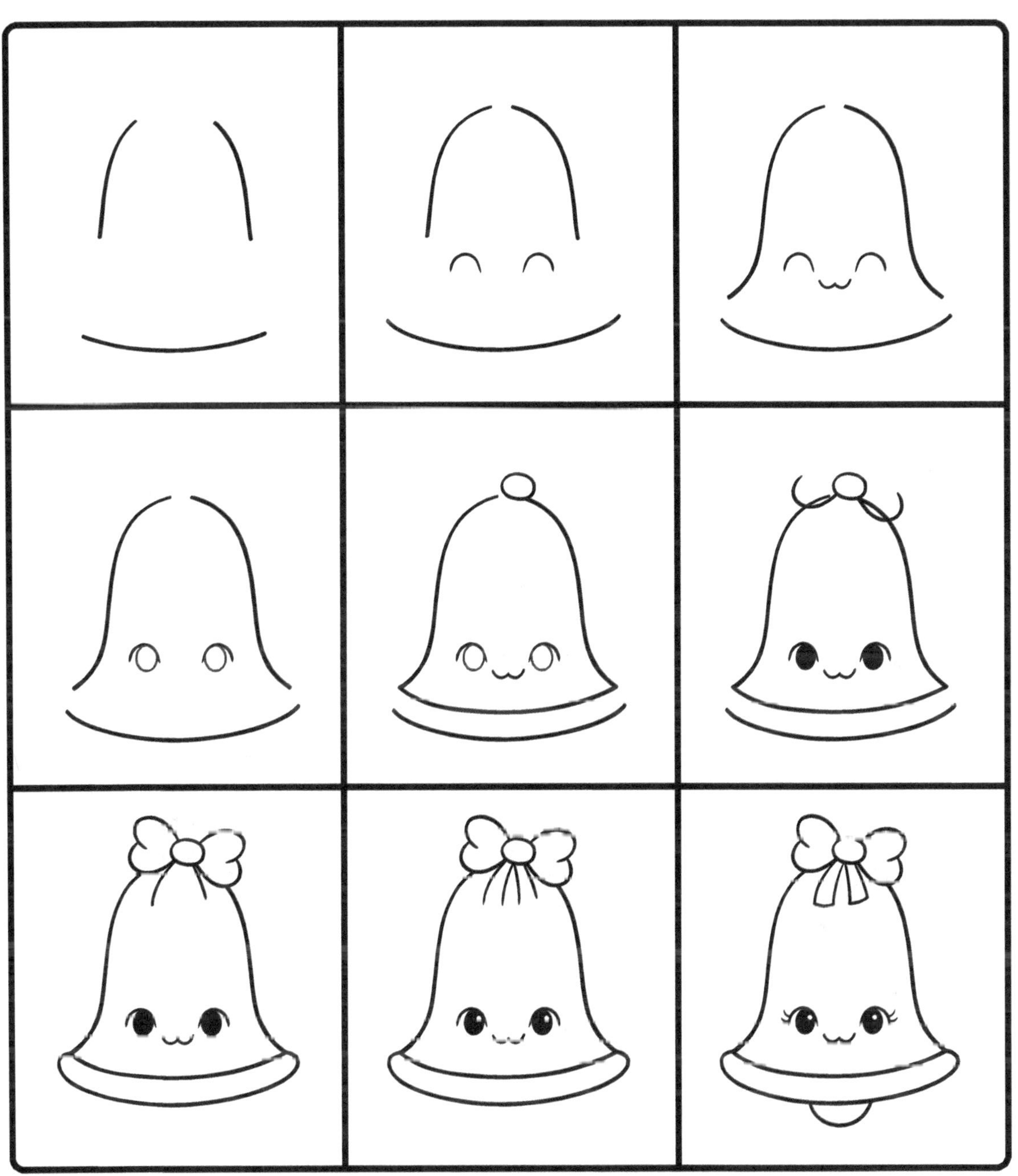

CANDIE

LIVES:
ON THE CHRISTMAS TREE.

LOVES MOST ABOUT CHRISTMAS:
SWINGING FROM BRANCH TO BRANCH
WHEN NO ONE IS LOOKING.

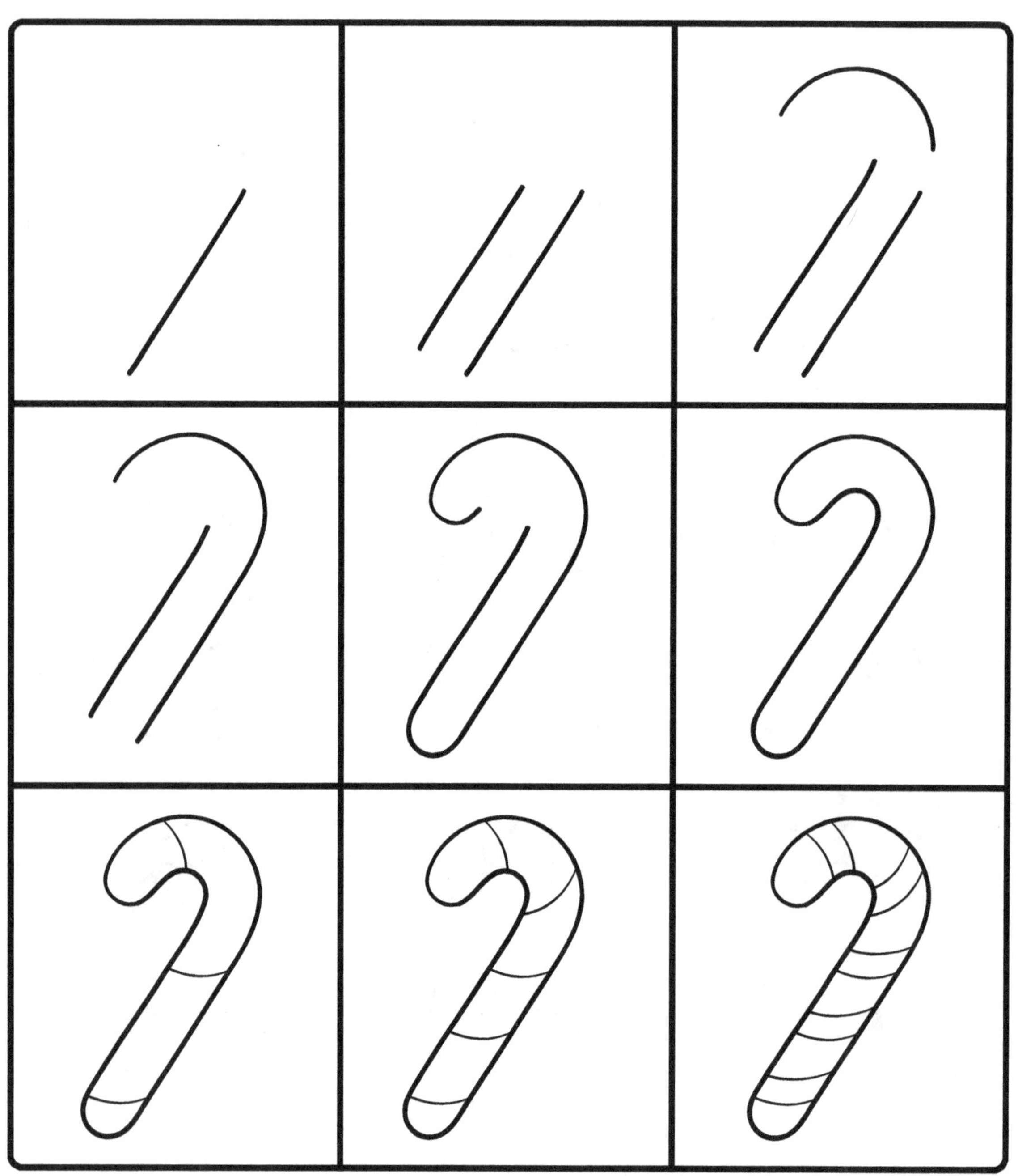

FLUFF

LIVES:
ON AN ICE SKATING RINK SIGN.

LOVES MOST ABOUT CHRISTMAS:
LISTENING TO PEOPLE LAUGH AS THEY
SKATE ROUND AND ROUND THE RINK.

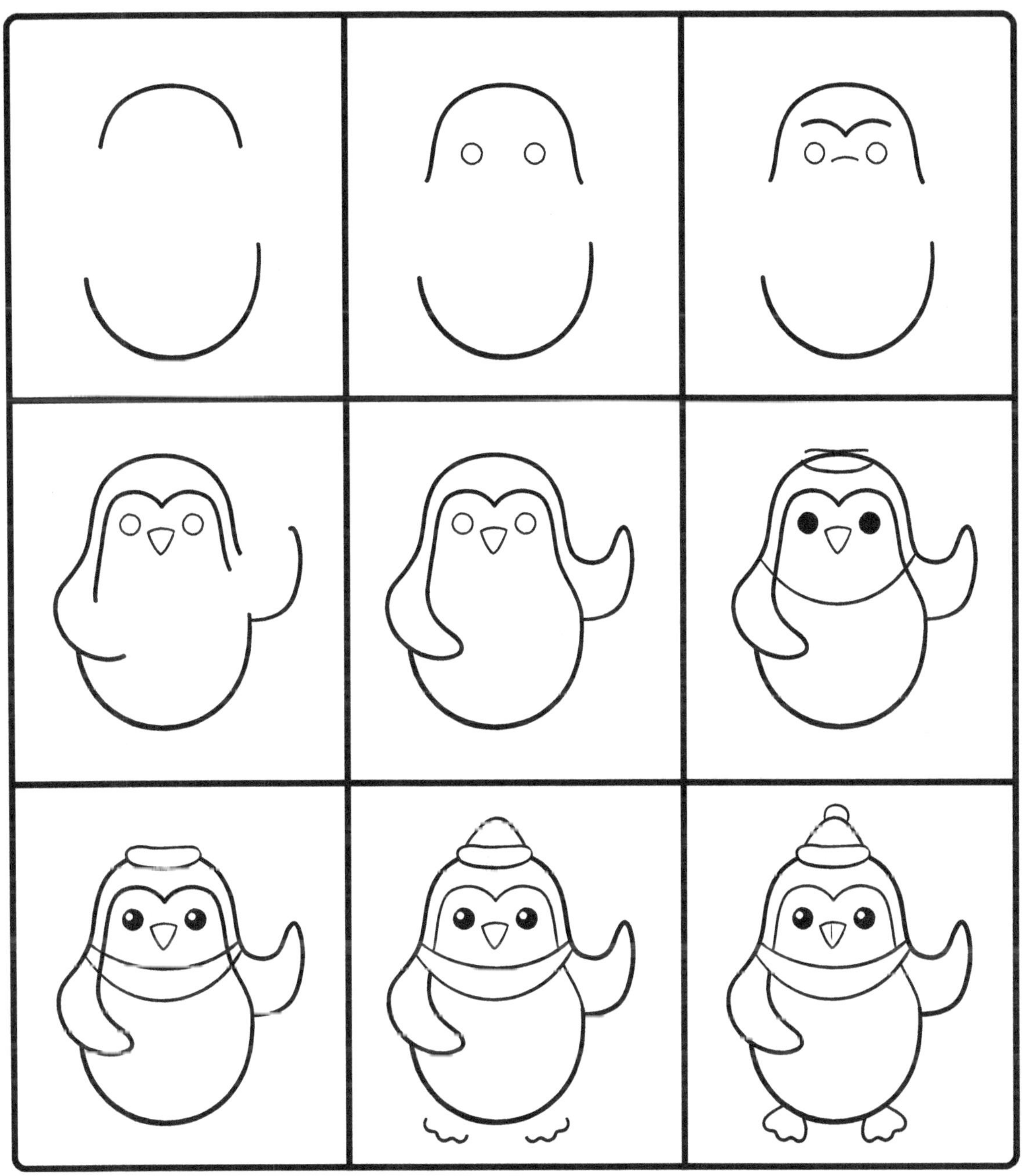

JOLLY

NEXT TO THE FIREPLACE ON CHRISTMAS MORNING.

THE SQUEALS OF EXCITEMENT AS THE TOYS AND GIFTS SPILL OUT OF HER.

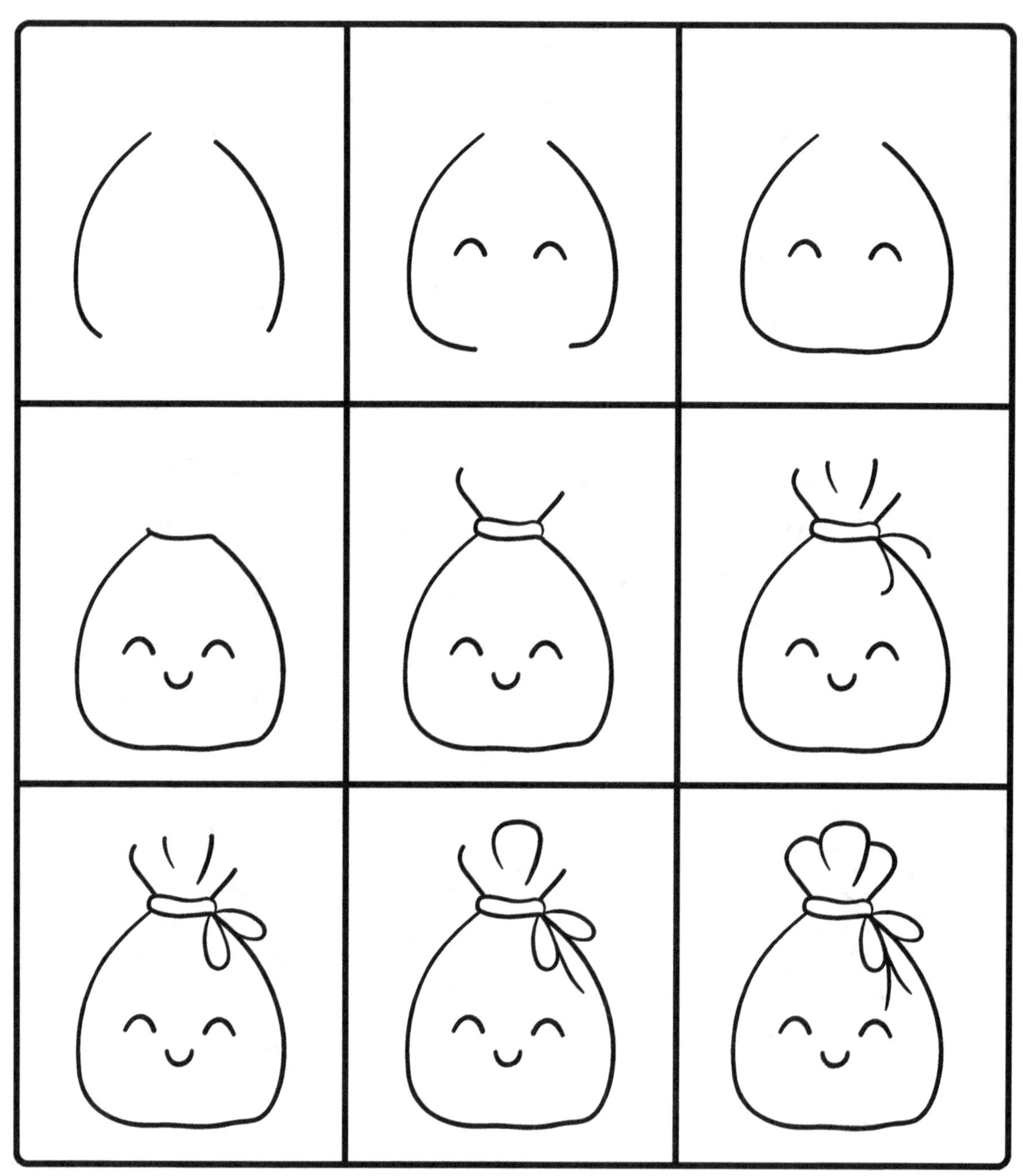

LIVES:

IN A LOCAL PARK, MADE WITH LITTLE HAPPY HANDS.

LOVES MOST ABOUT CHRISTMAS:

WATCHING SNOWBALL FIGHTS ALL AROUND HIM.

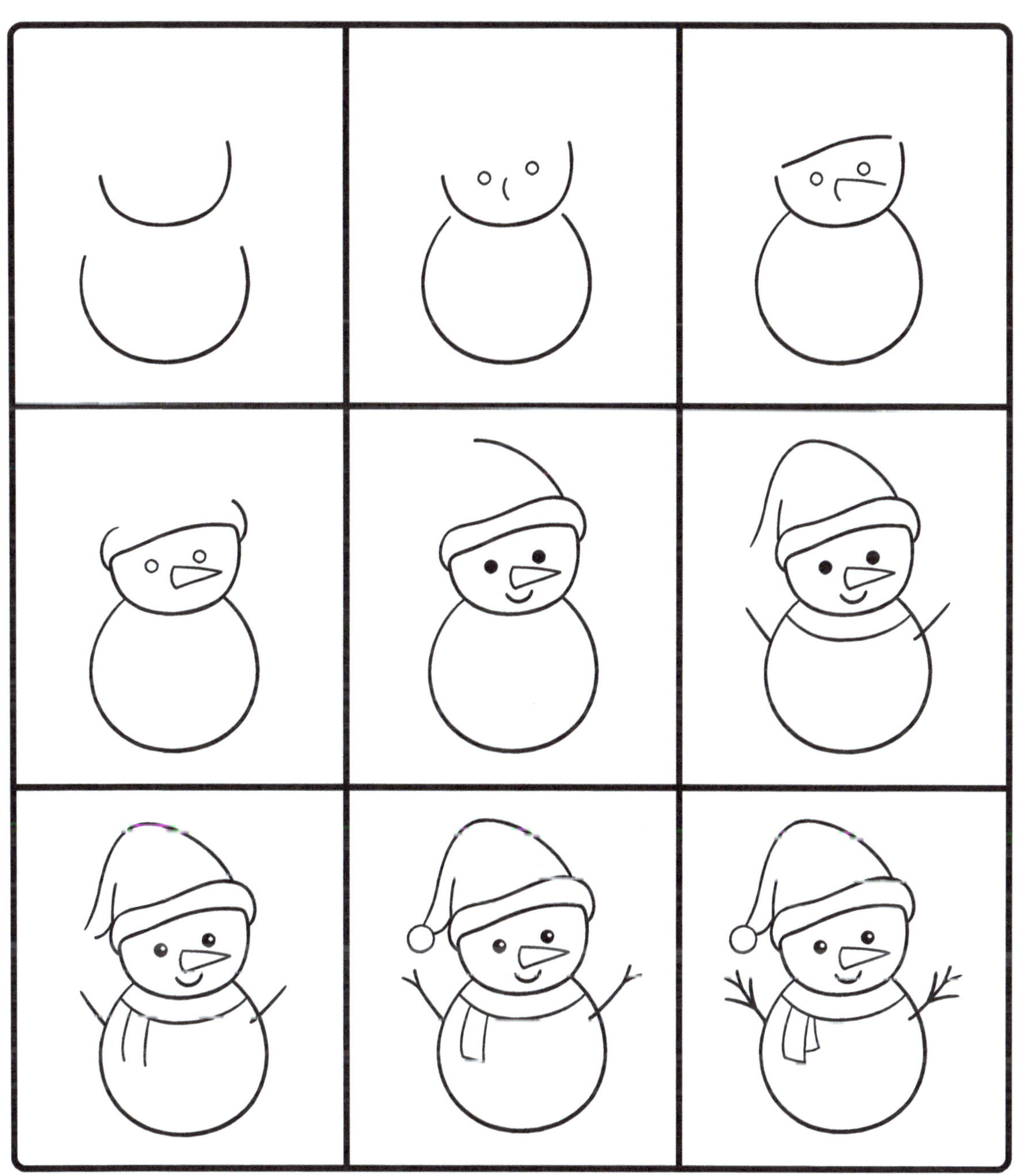

SNUGGLY

WRAPPED UP UNDER THE TREE, NEXT TO THE SNOW GLOBE BOX.

KEEPING TUMMIES WARM ON THE BIG DAY.

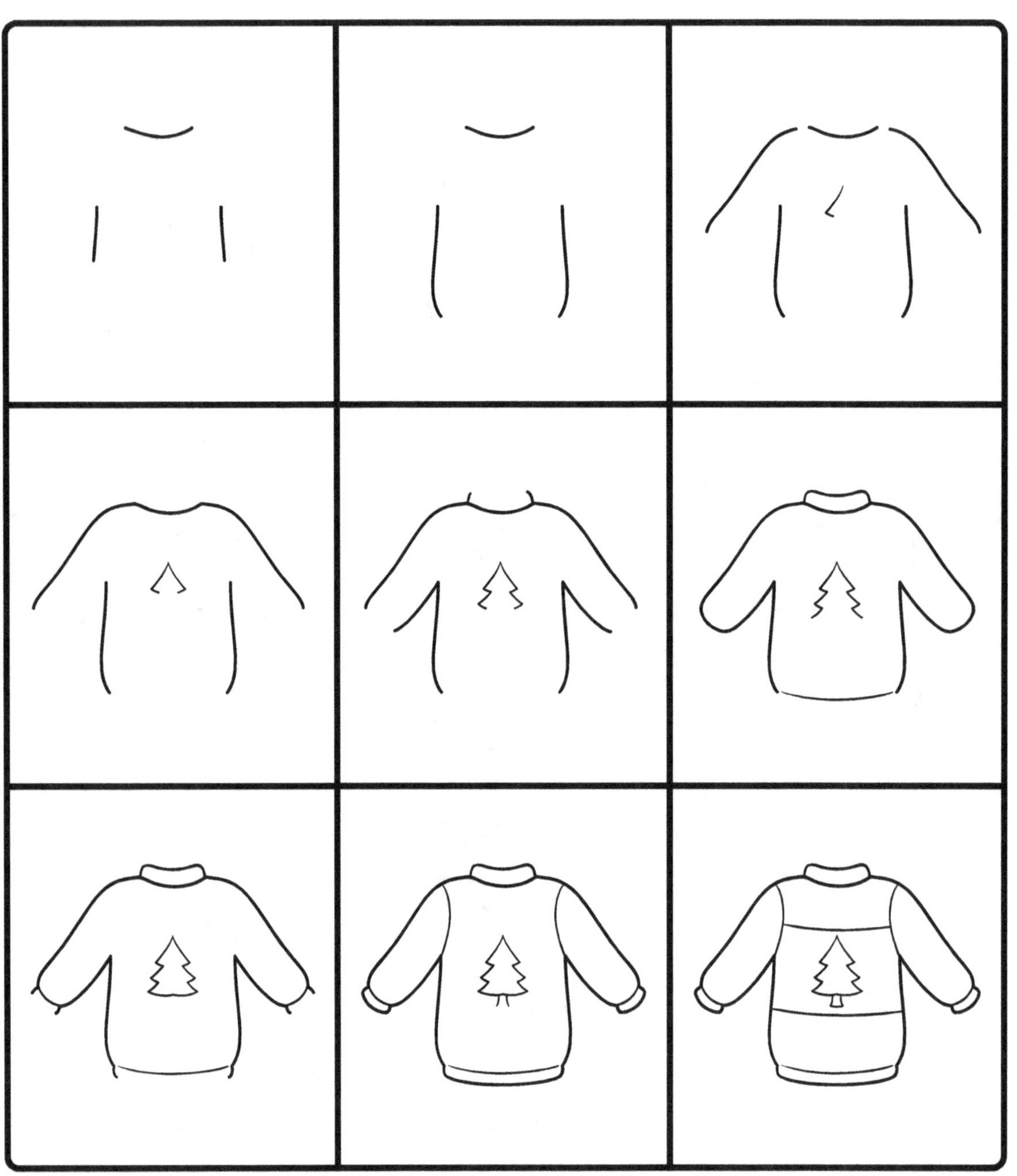

SANTA CLAUS

LIVES:
AT THE NORTH POLE.

LOVES MOST ABOUT CHRISTMAS:
SOARING THROUGH THE COLD WINTER
AIR, DELIVERING GIFTS TO ALL OF THE
KIDS AROUND THE WORLD.

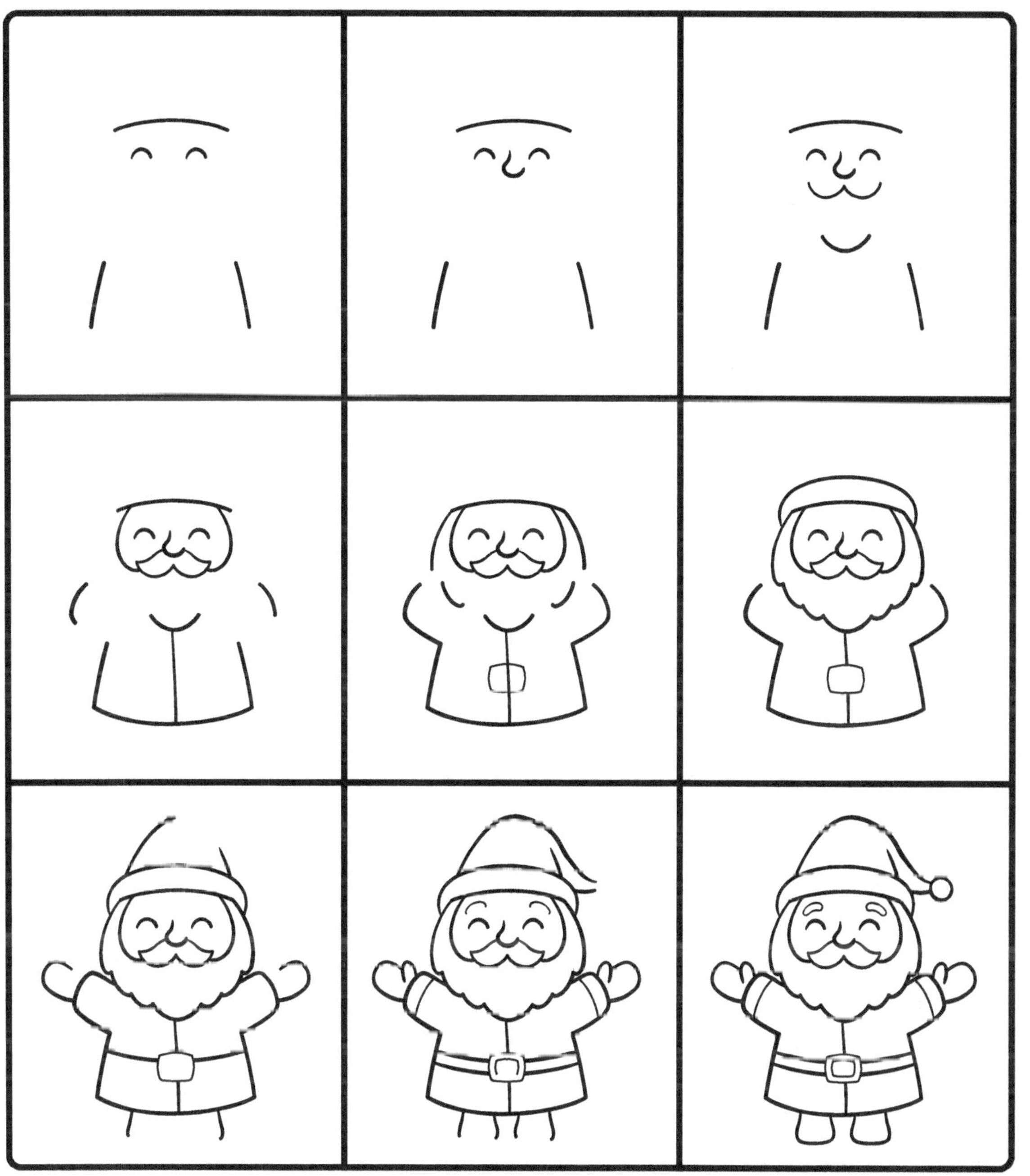

LUMI

LIVES:
ON THE COUNTER OF A TINY BOOK STORE.

LOVES MOST ABOUT CHRISTMAS:
HOW BUSY THE SHOP BECOMES AROUND CHRISTMAS TIME.

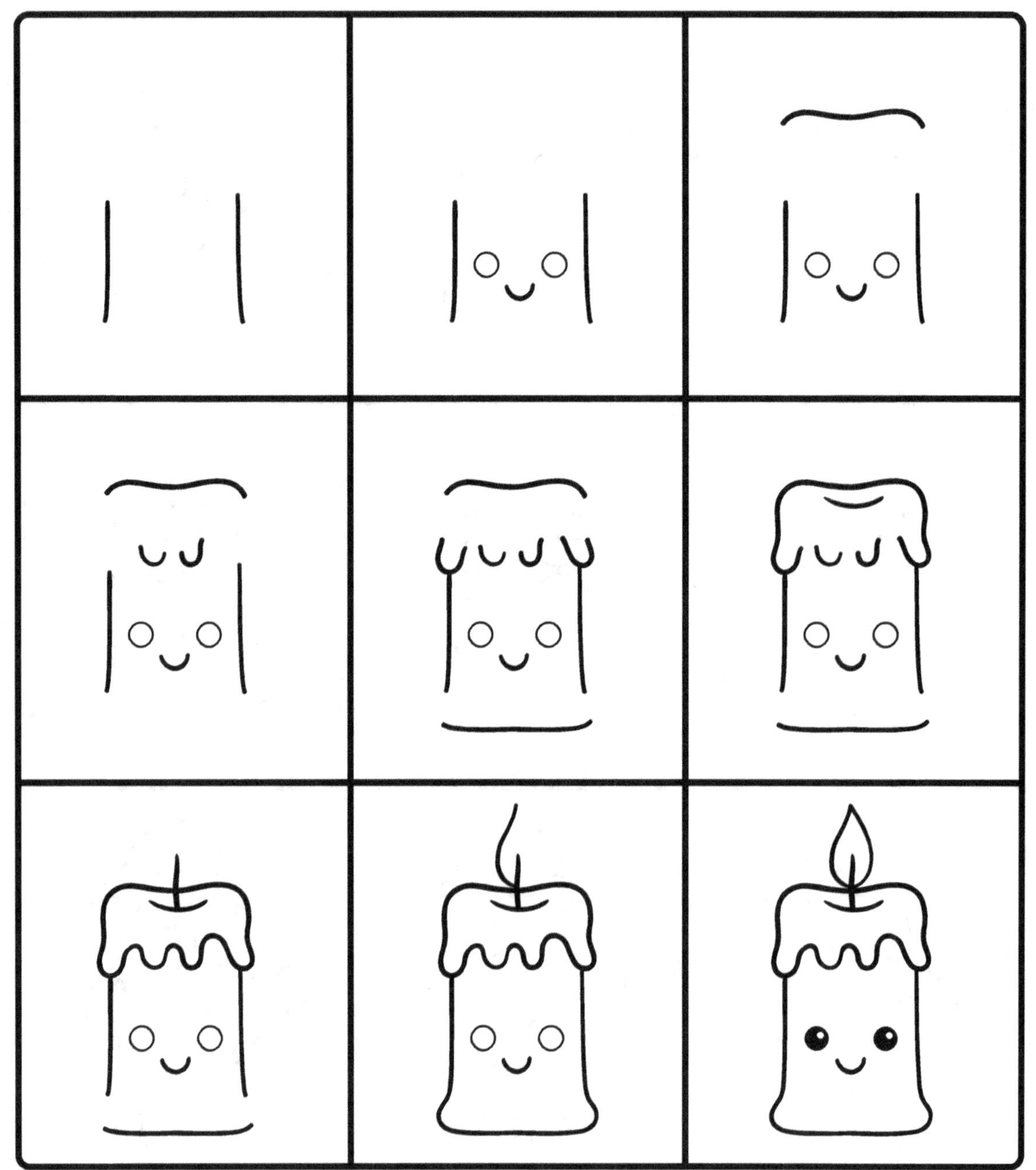

SPICE

ON A BEAUTIFULLY DECORATED CHRISTMAS TABLE WAITING TO BE SIPPED.

BEING SIPPED AND ENJOYED.

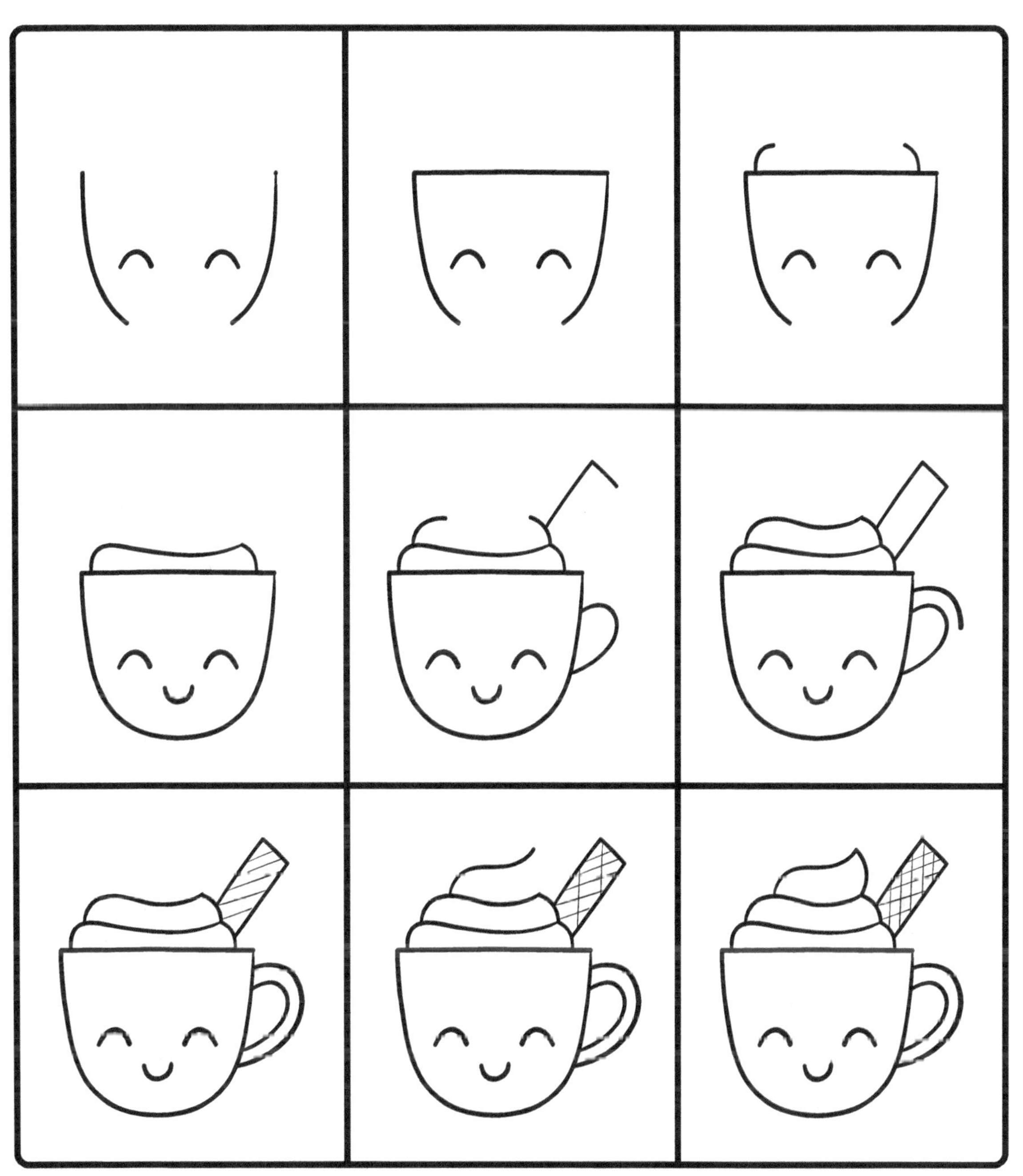

ALFIE

IN SANTA'S WORKSHOP, BUSILY MAKING BEAUTIFUL GIFTS.

LOVES MOST ABOUT CHRISTMAS:
PAINTING, CREATING, AND DECORATING WITH HIS ELF PALS.

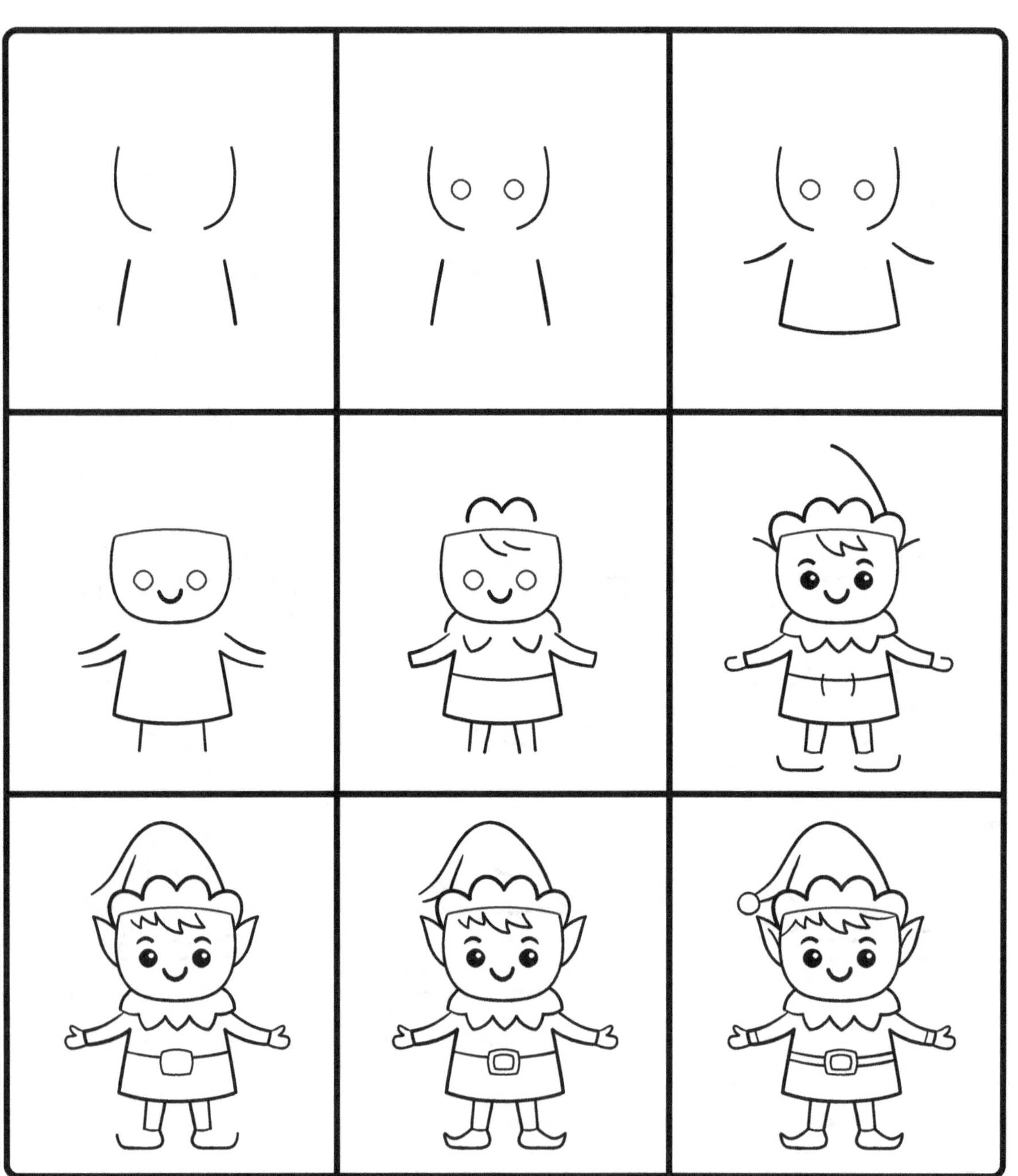

TEDDYKIN

LIVES:
IN THE ARMS OF A VERY LITTLE EXCITED
GIRL ON CHRISTMAS EVE.

LOVES MOST ABOUT CHRISTMAS:
LISTENING TO SANTA'S SLEIGH BELLS
TINKLE AS IT ARRIVES.

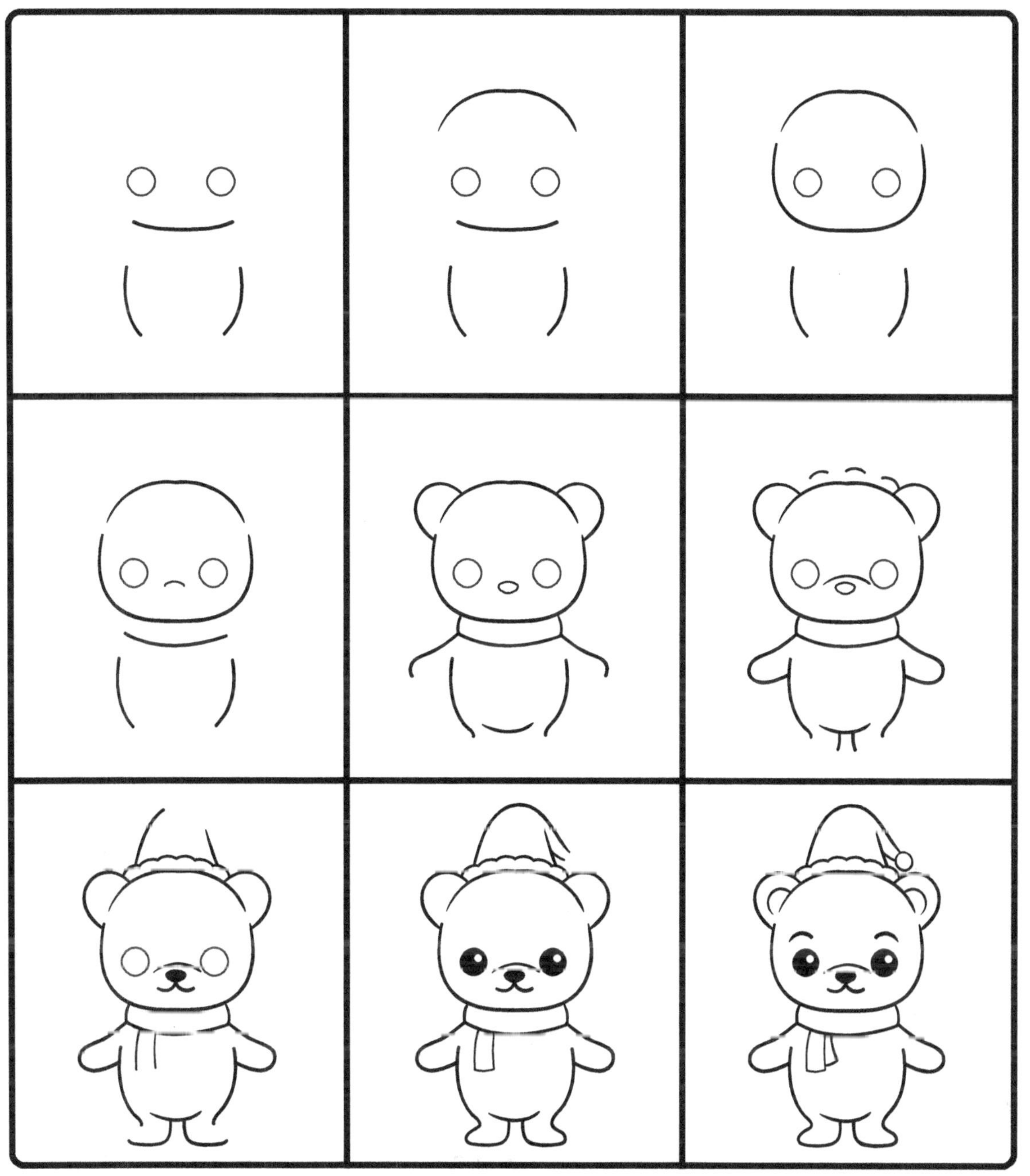

REINDEAR

IN A STABLE IN THE NORTH POLE, NOT FAR FROM SANTA'S HOME.

THE WIND IN HIS FUR AS HE FLIES SANTA ALL AROUND THE WORLD DELIVERING GIFTS.

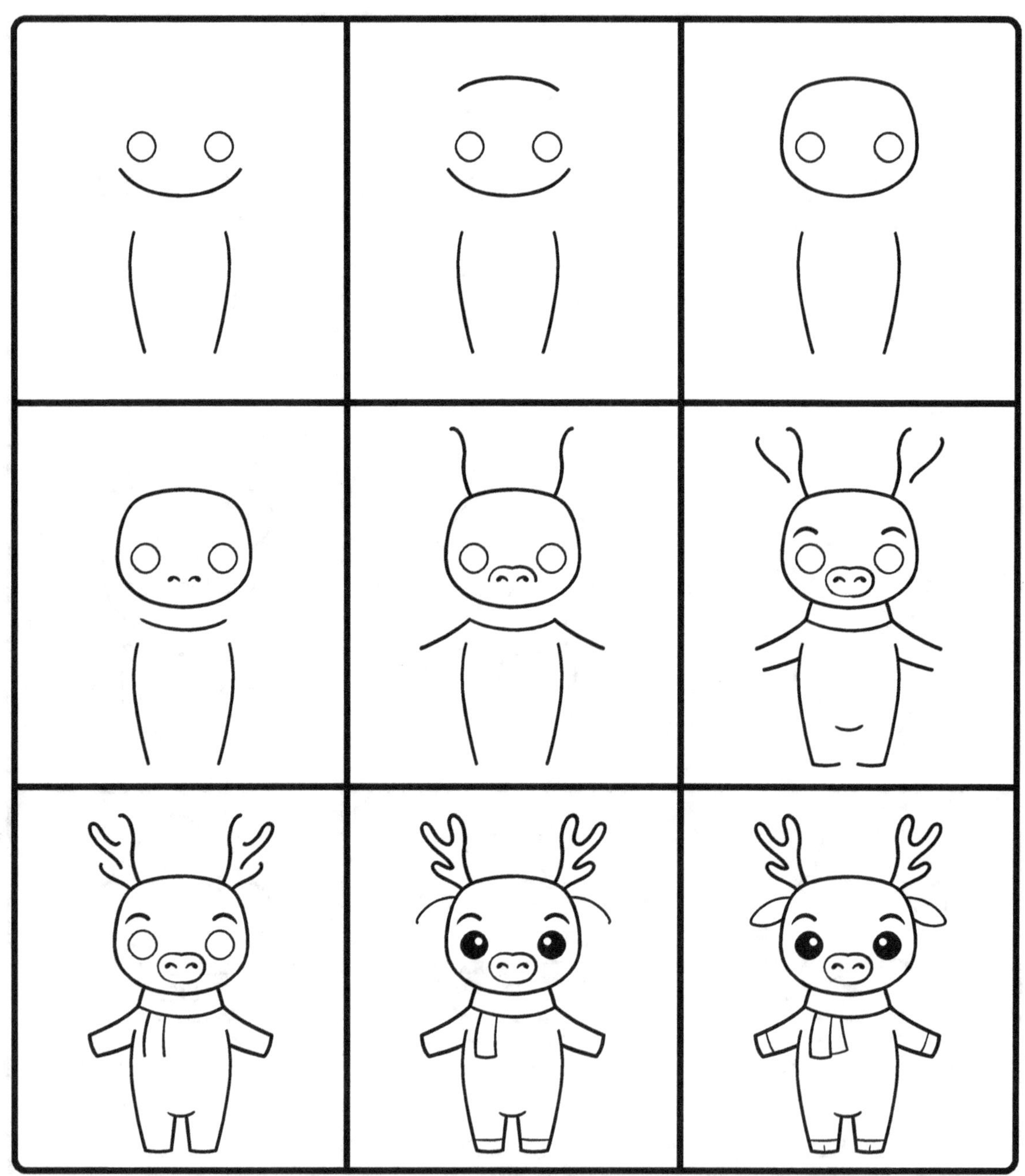

ON THE FRONT DOOR OF A RED-PAINTED DOOR.

BEING MADE! CREATED OUT OF LEAVES, TWIGS, AND COLORFUL BERRIES.

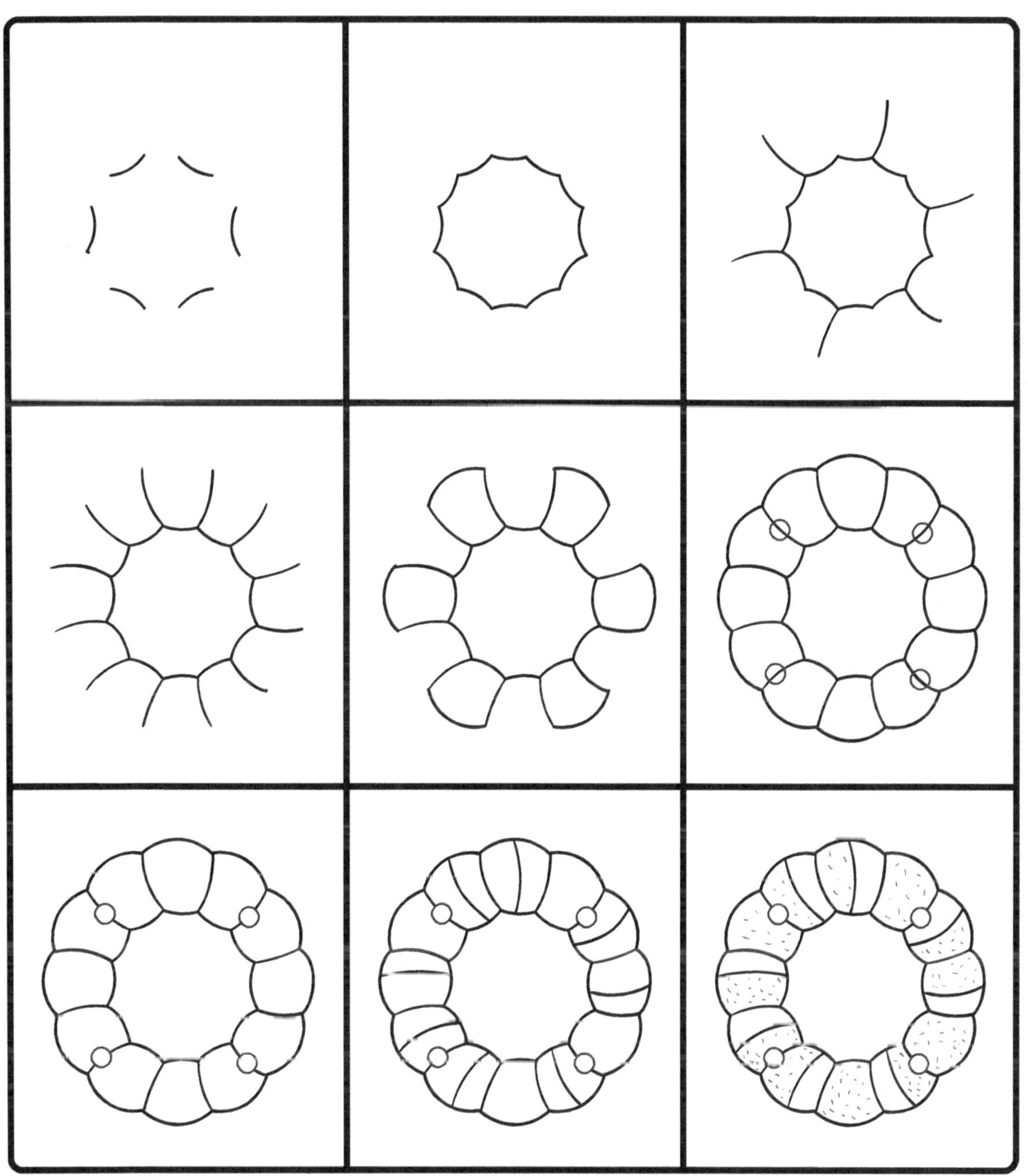

WOOLLIE

ON TOP OF A LITTLE BOY'S HEAD AS HE WALKS TO SCHOOL ON COLD SNOWY MORNINGS.

KEEPING THE LITTLE BOY WARM AT THE MOST SPECIAL TIME OF THE YEAR.

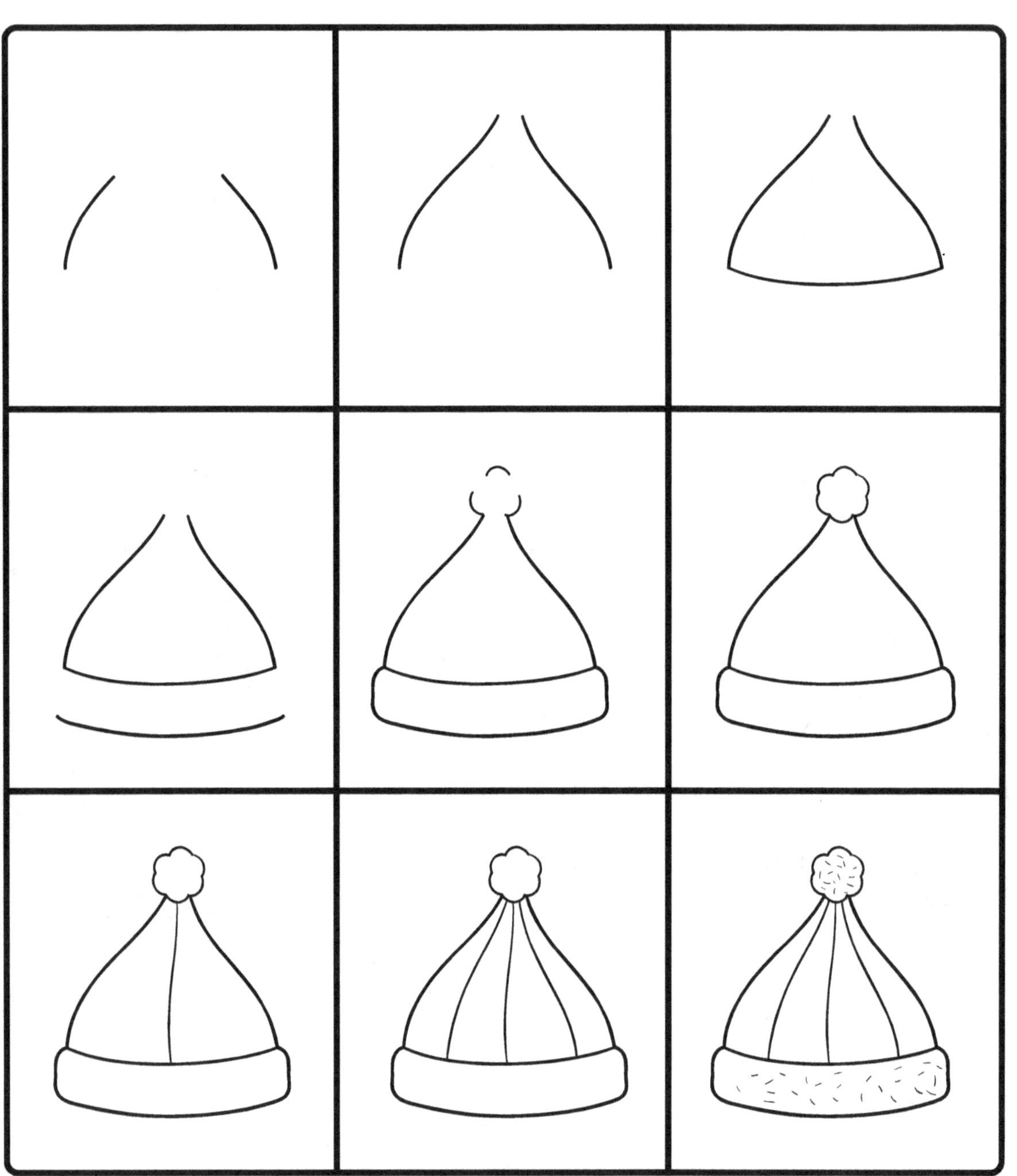

CHRISTMAS CANDY POP

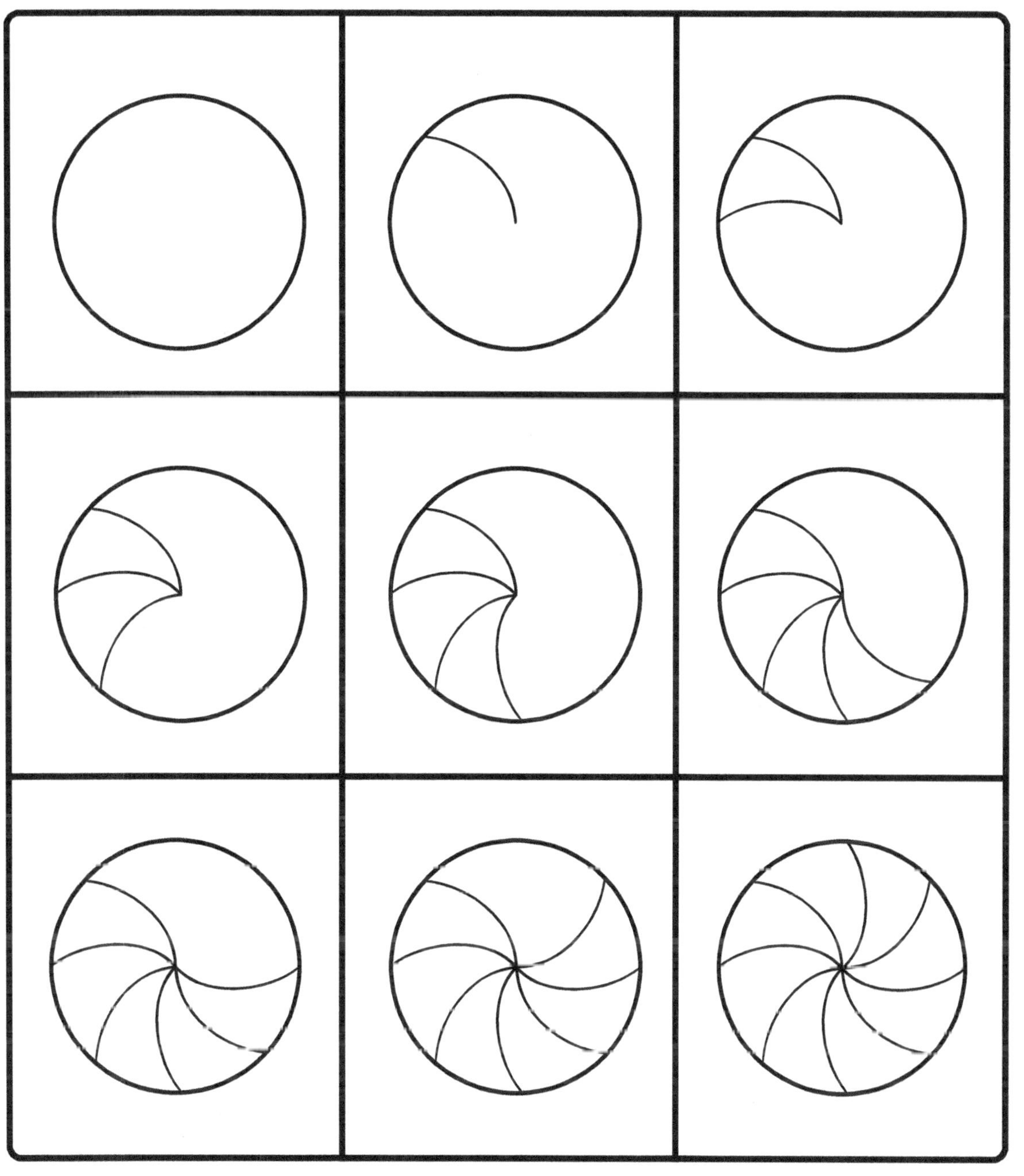

PUD

LIVES:
RIGHT IN THE MIDDLE OF THE CHRISTMAS TABLE READY TO BE SERVED TO A BIG HAPPY FAMILY.

LOVES MOST ABOUT CHRISTMAS:
THE 'OOOHS' AND 'AAAHS' WHEN PEOPLE TAKE A BITE OF HIM.

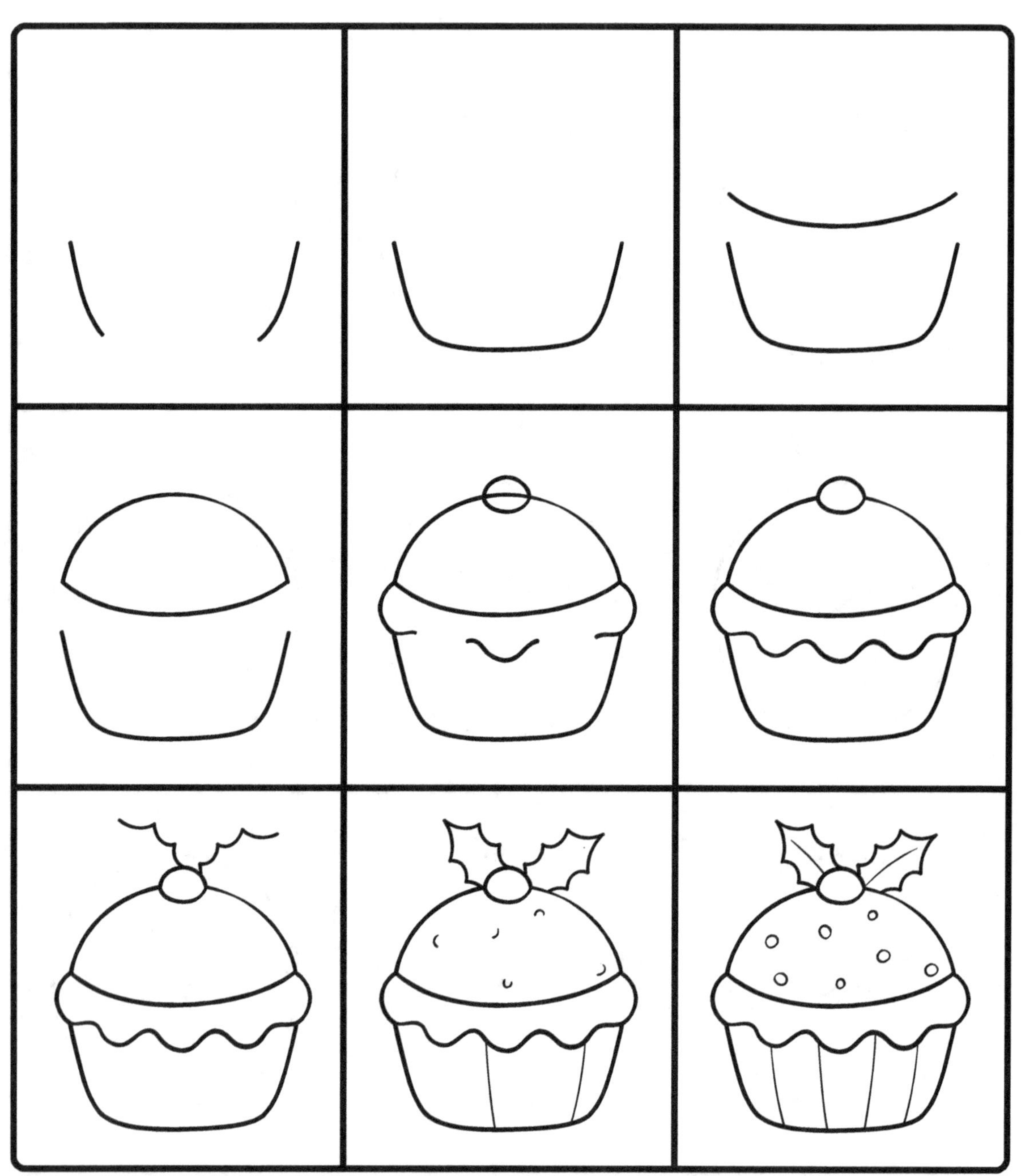

VANILLY

LIVES:
IN AN ICE CREAM VAN.

LOVES MOST ABOUT CHRISTMAS:
LOOKING OUT THE WINDOW AS THE
VAN DRIVES PAST ALL THE BEAUTIFUL
CHRISTMAS LIGHTS, LIGHTING UP THE
WHOLE TOWN.

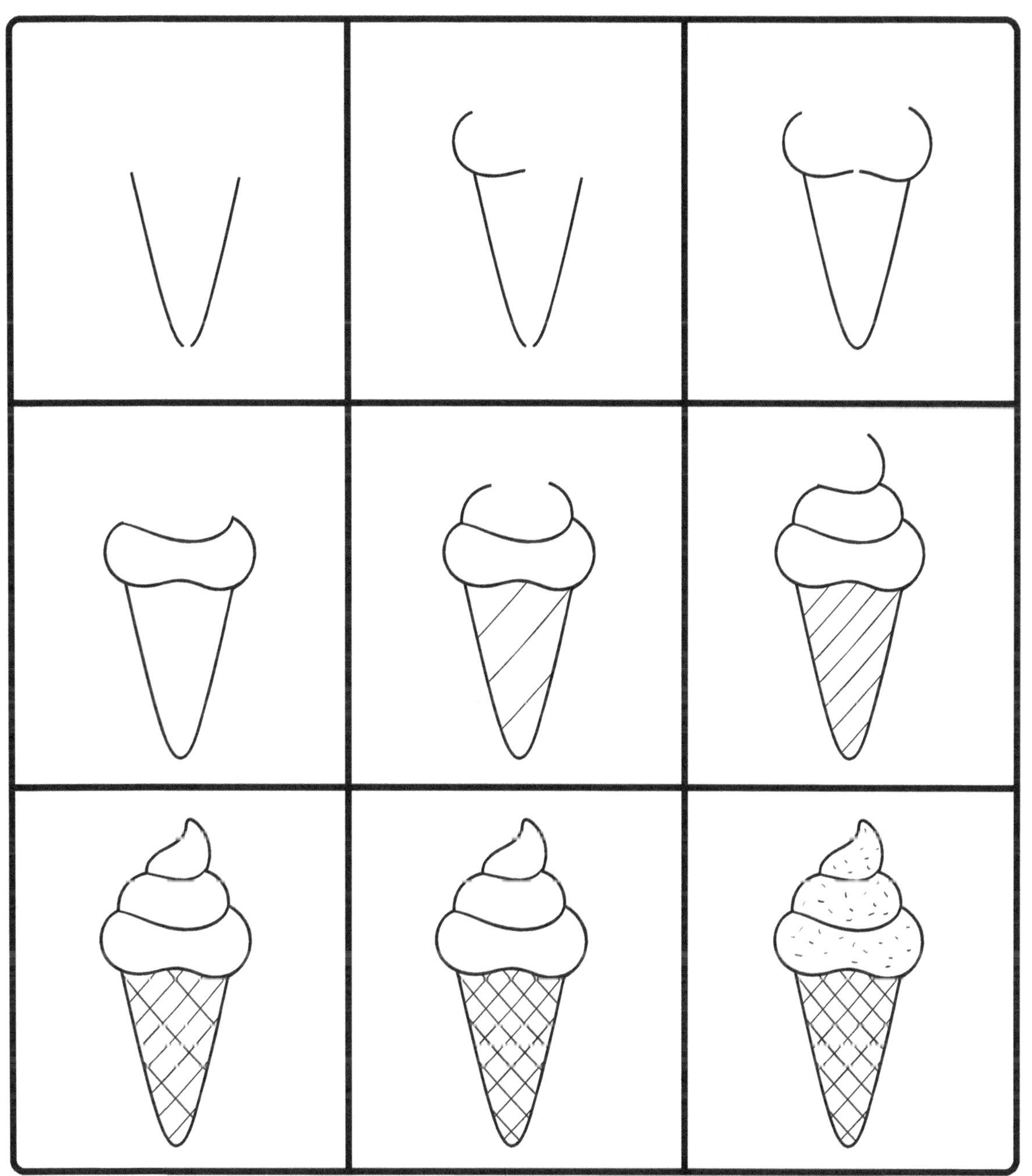

CANDY SNAP

LIVES:
IN A BOX, WAITING TO BE MADE.

LOVES MOST ABOUT CHRISTMAS:
WHEN SHE'S ALL MADE AND IT'S TIME FOR
COVERING HER IN CANDY!

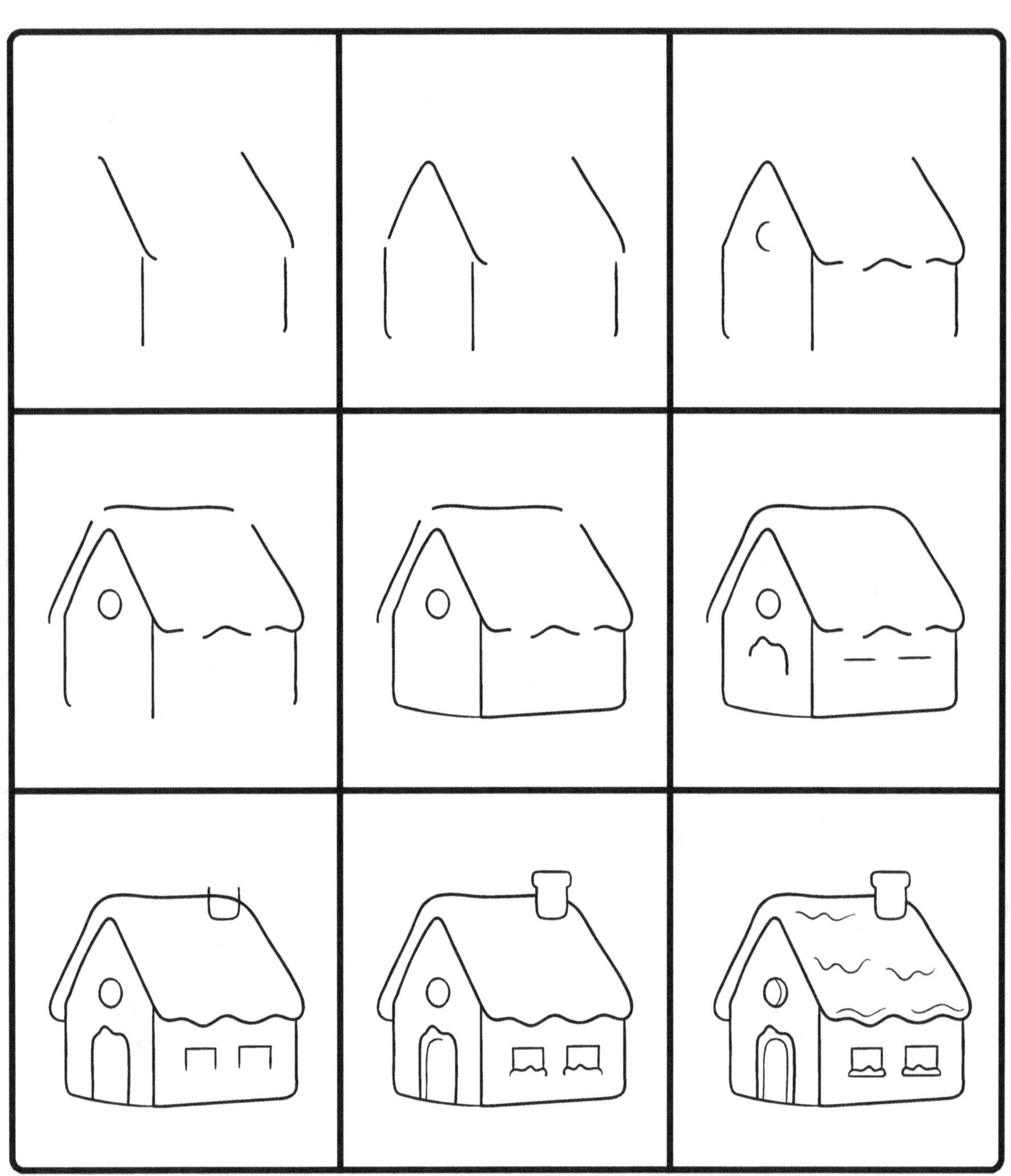

SNOW MONSTER

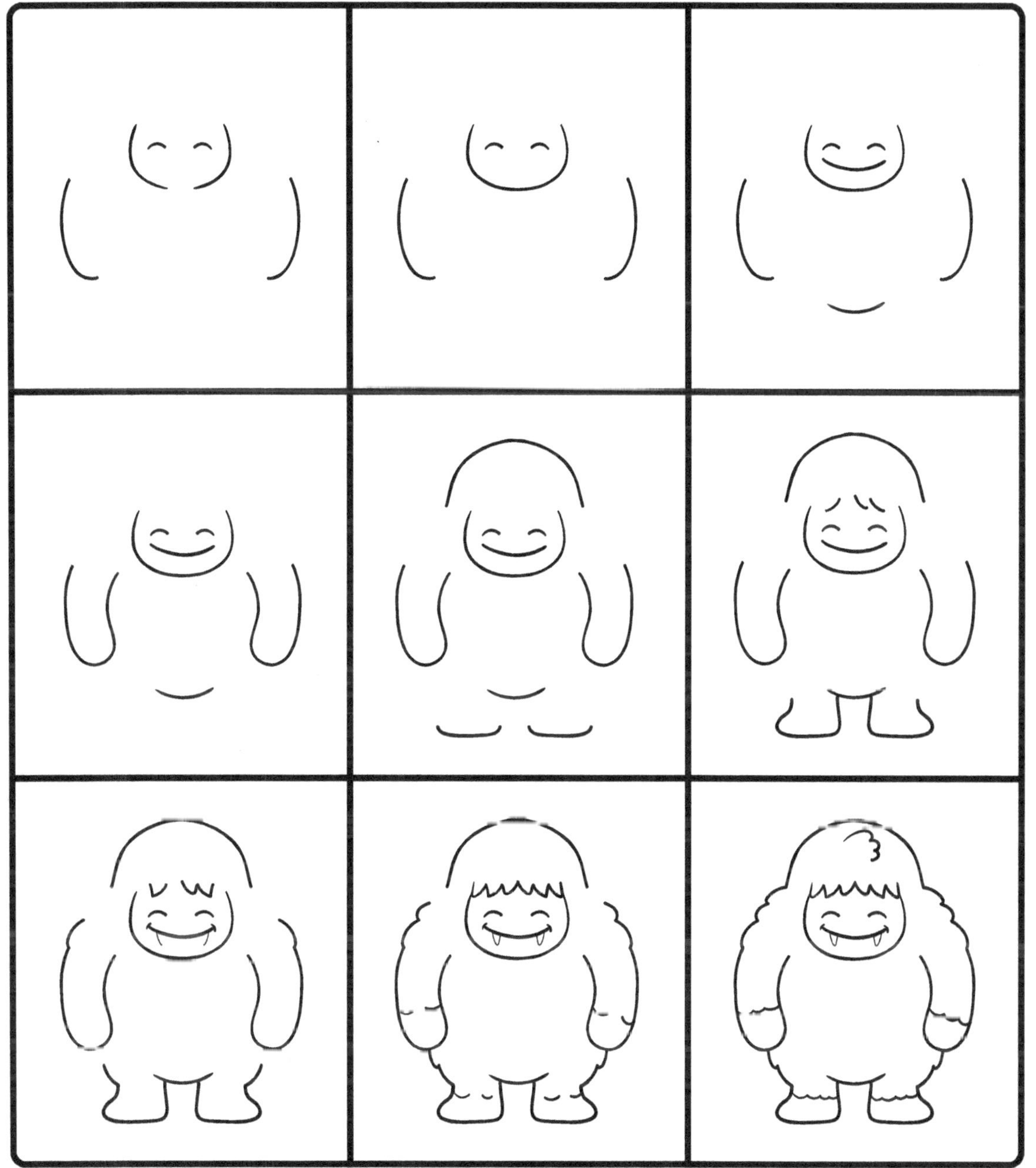

SHORTCAKE

LIVES:
IN A COFFEE SHOP IN A BUSY SHOPPING MALL.

LOVES MOST ABOUT CHRISTMAS:
PEOPLE ADMIRING HER IN THE GLASS CASE AS THEY GO ABOUT THEIR SHOPPING.

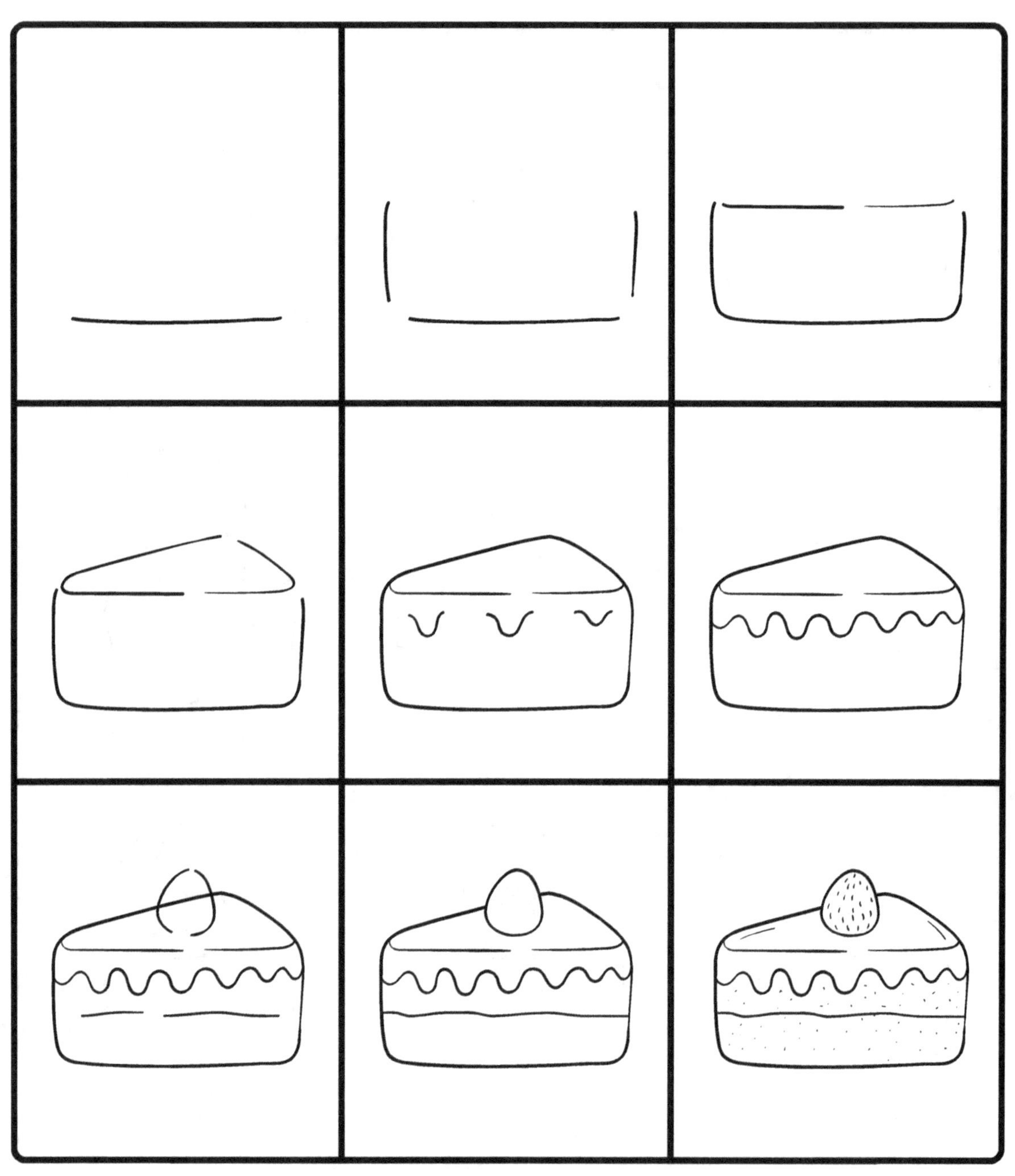

PINEY

ON A CHRISTMAS TREE FARM, WAITING TO BE CUT DOWN AND PLACED LOVINGLY IN SOMEONE'S HOME TO BE DECORATED.

BEING COVERED IN TINSEL, ORNAMENTS AND A STAR RIGHT ON HER TIP.

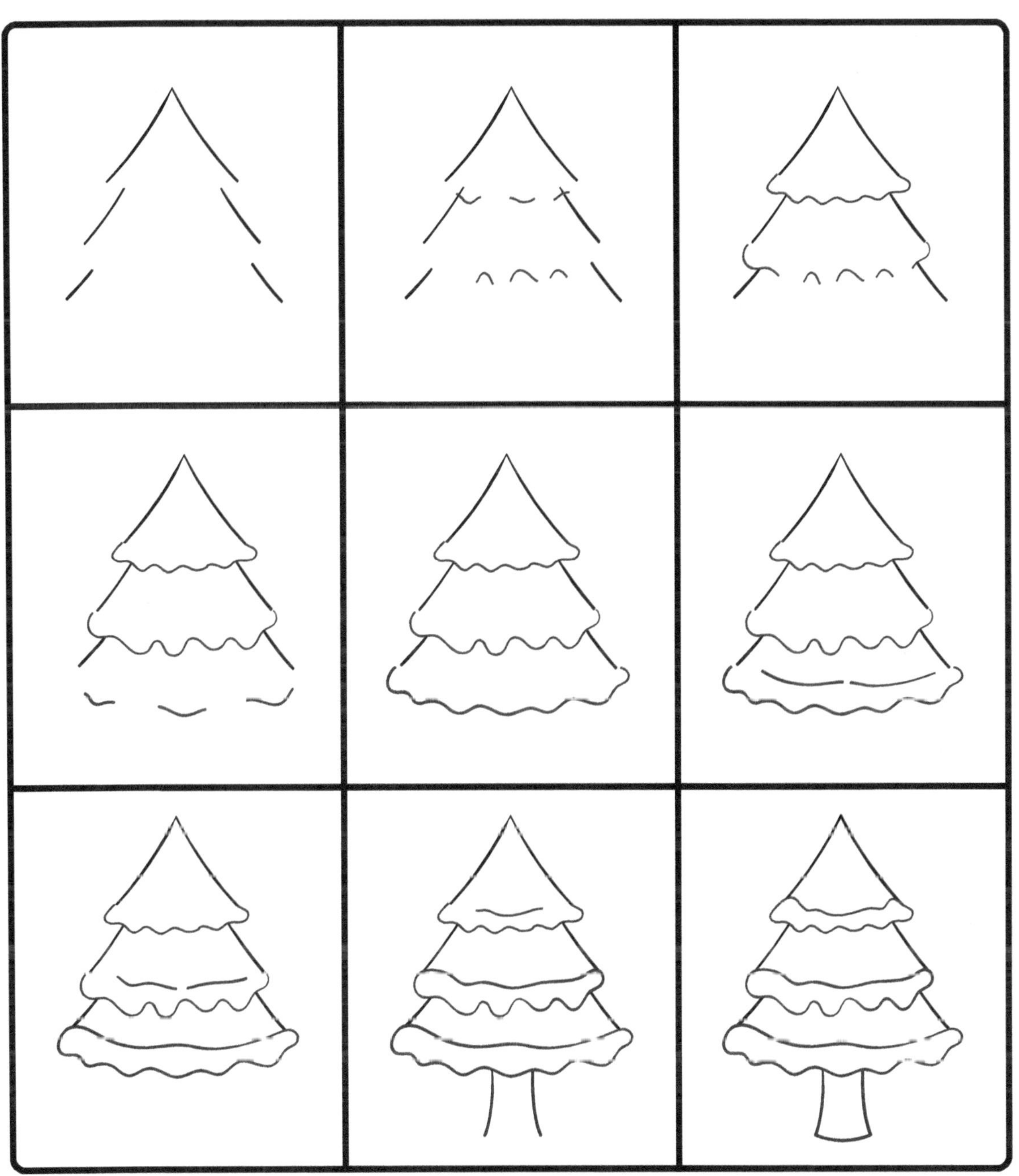

LIVES:
WRAPPED UP IN A BOX UNDER THE CHRISTMAS TREE.

LOVES MOST ABOUT CHRISTMAS:
THE FIRST SHAKE, SHAKING, SHAKING OF HIS SNOW.

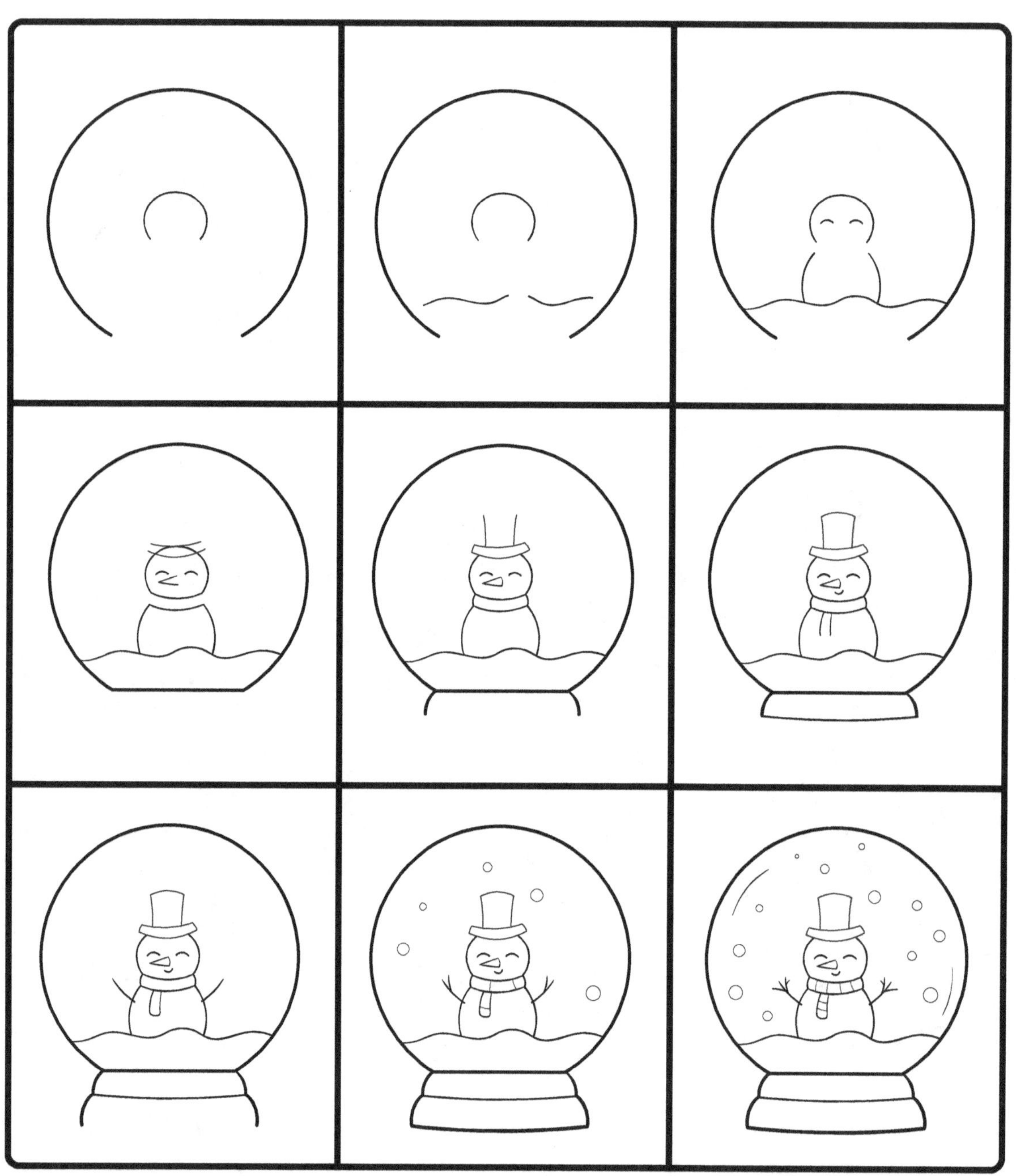

CHRISSY KOALA

IN A GUM TREE IN A BIG YARD NEXT TO A BUSY, SPLASHY SWIMMING POOL.

THAT IT'S WARM AND SUNNY IN AUSTRALIA.

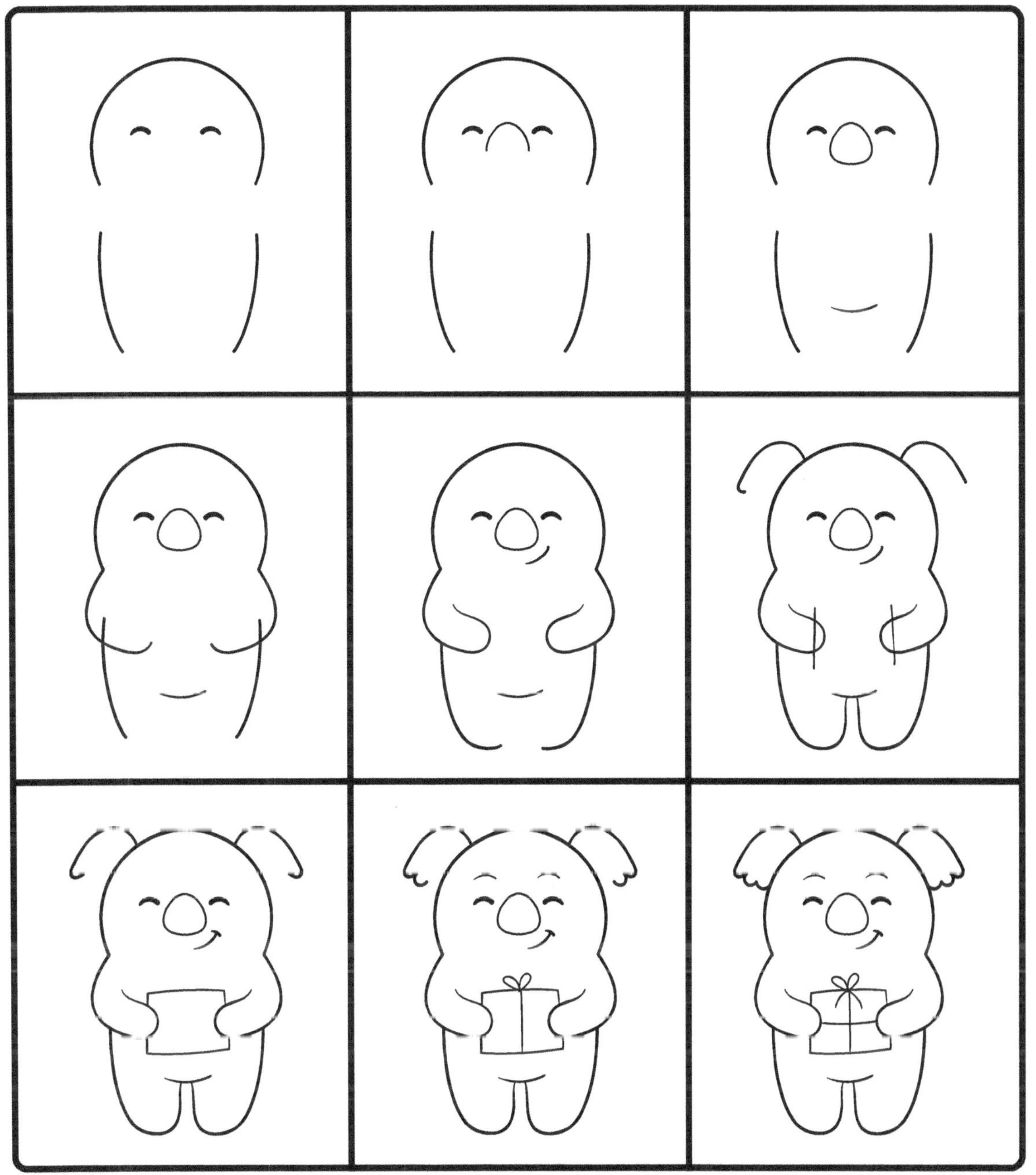

PLUM

LIVES:
WRAPPED UP IN A SCHOOLBAG, READY TO
BE GIFTED TO A CHILD'S TEACHER FOR
CHRISTMAS.

LOVES MOST ABOUT CHRISTMAS:
LISTENING TO CAROLS BEING PLAYED
WHILE BEING MADE.

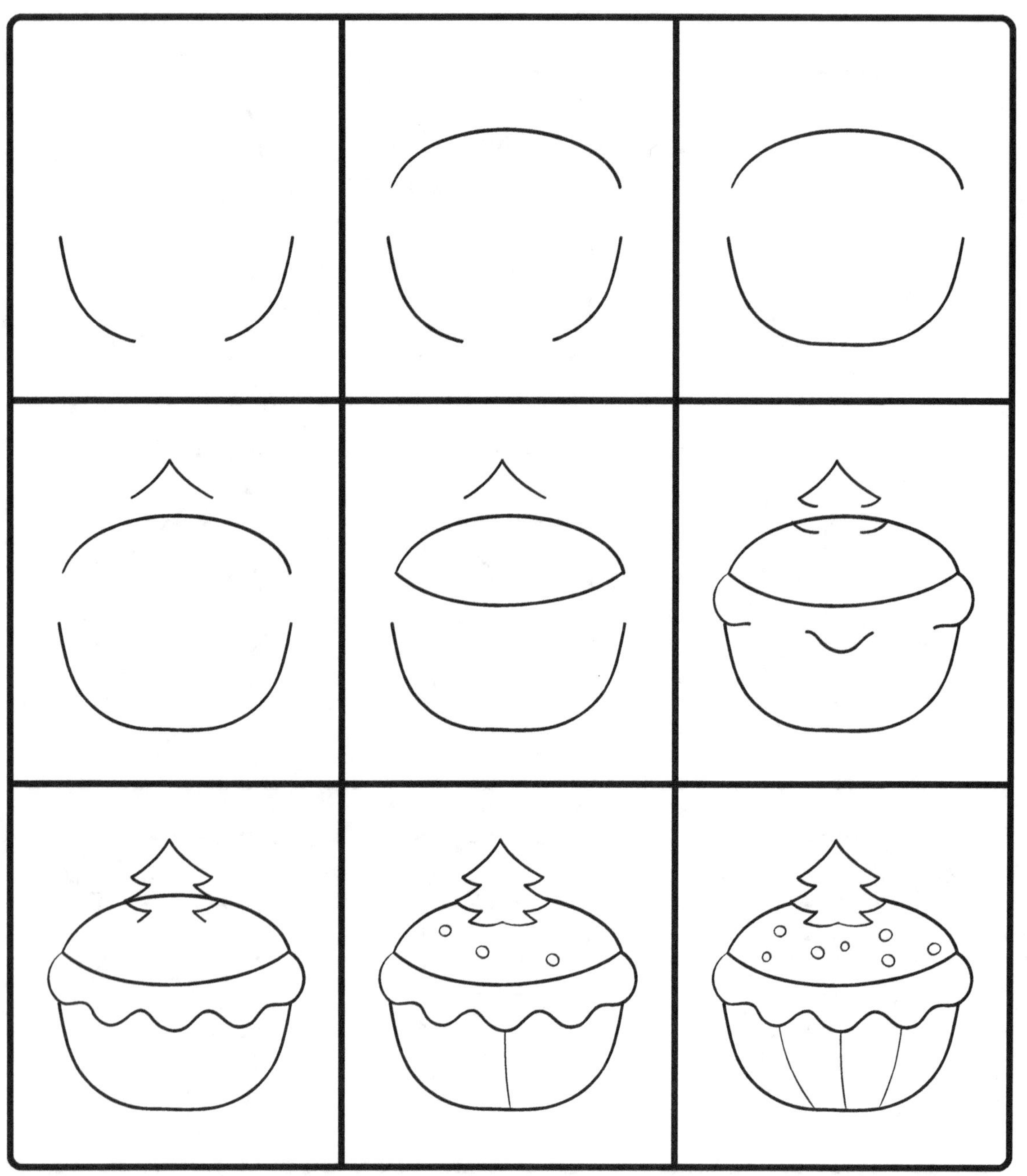

CRYSTAL

LIVES:
IN THE SKY, SPARKLING IN THE SUN, AS IT FLOATS, FLOATS, FLOATS SOFTLY DOWN TO THE GROUND.

LOVES MOST ABOUT CHRISTMAS:
CHILDREN POINTING OUT TO HER AS SHE FLOATS THROUGH THE AIR.

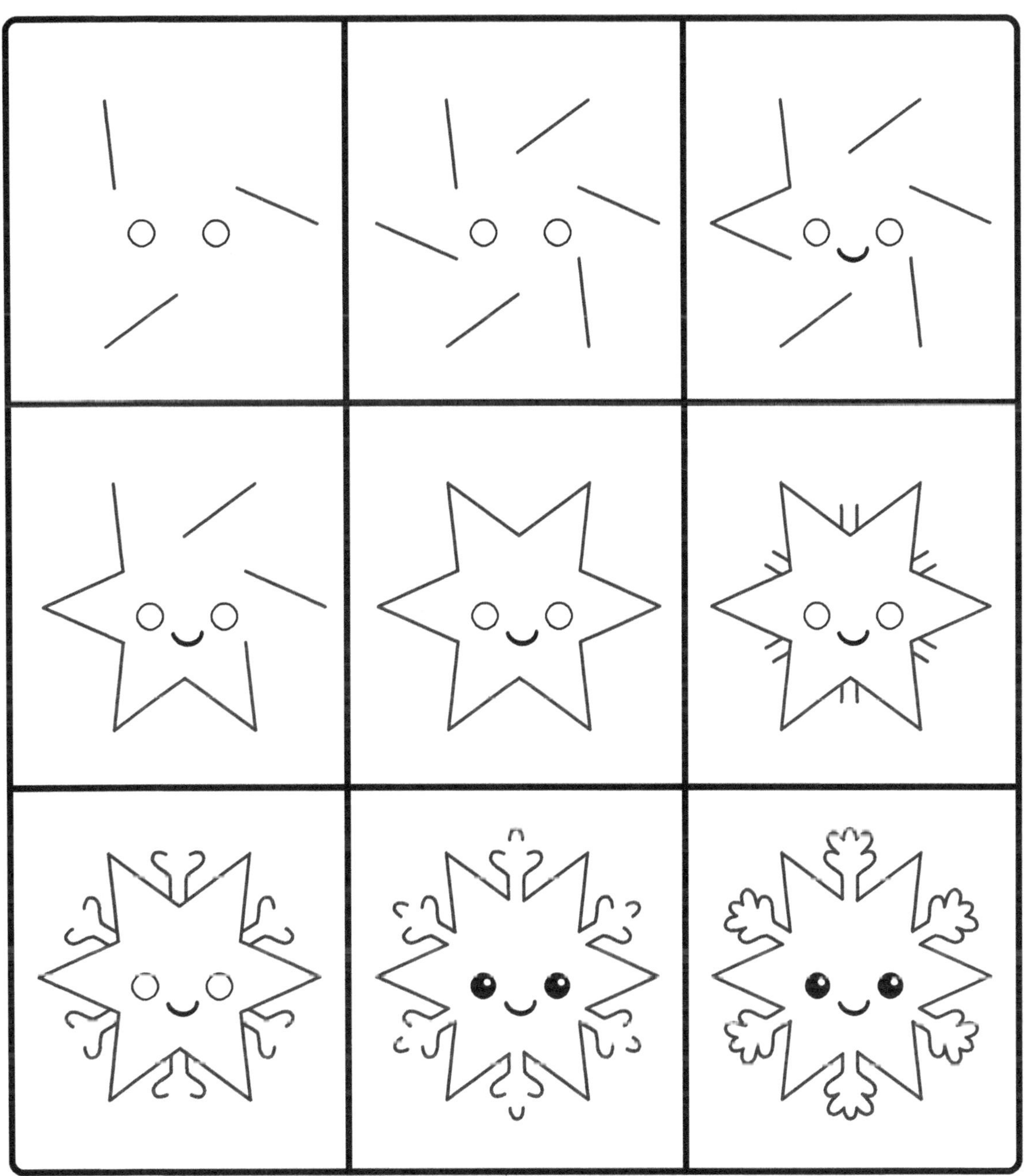

POINTY

LIVES:
ON A KITCHEN BENCHTOP.

LOVES MOST ABOUT CHRISTMAS:
WATCHING THE CHRISTMAS FEAST BEING PREPARED AND ENJOYING THE DELICIOUS SMELLS COMING FROM THE KITCHEN.

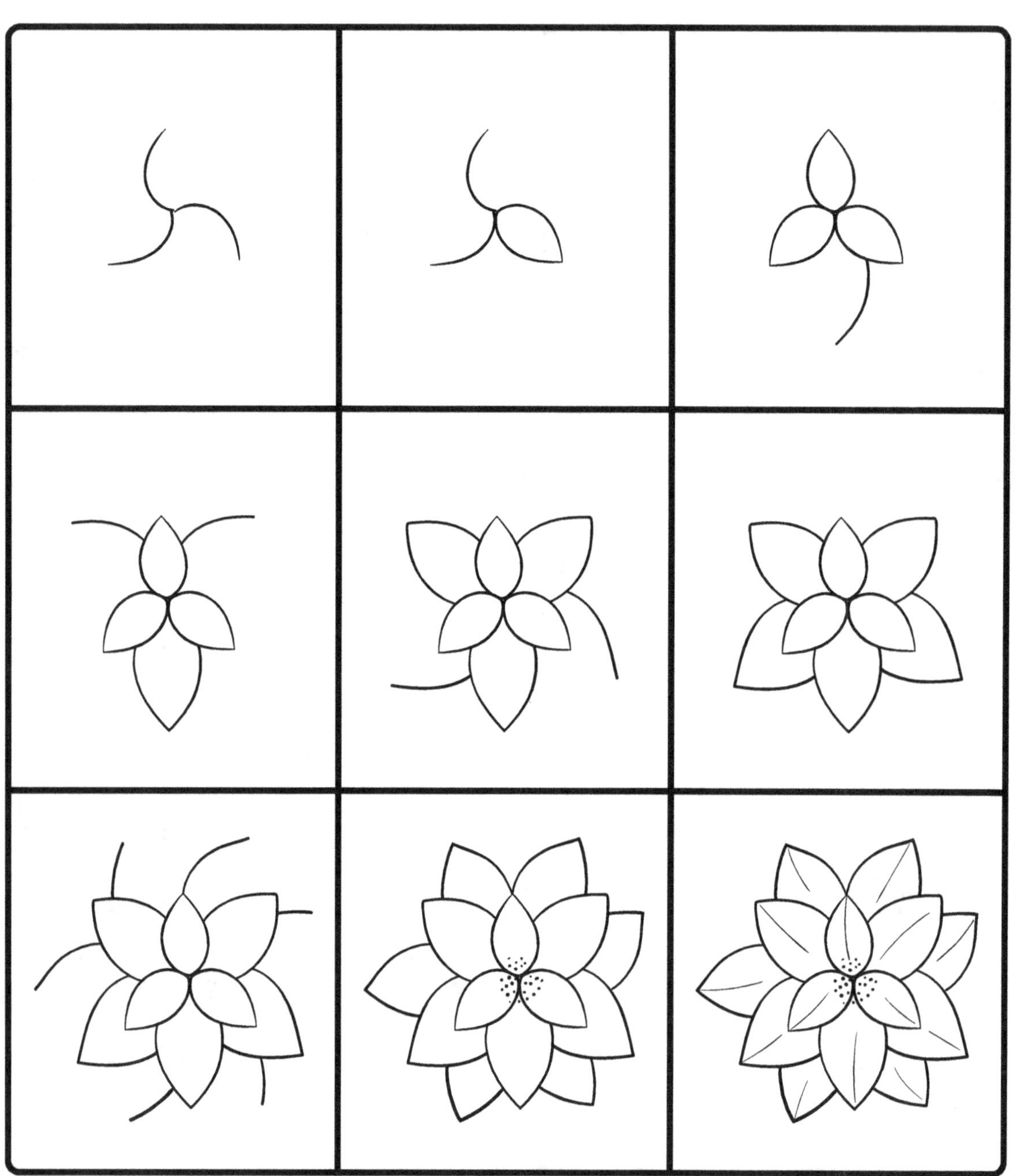

JOY-JOY

LIVES:
ON A CARD, STANDING ON A MANTLEPIECE.
LOVES MOST ABOUT CHRISTMAS:
READING ALL THE OTHER CARD'S HAPPY MESSAGES.

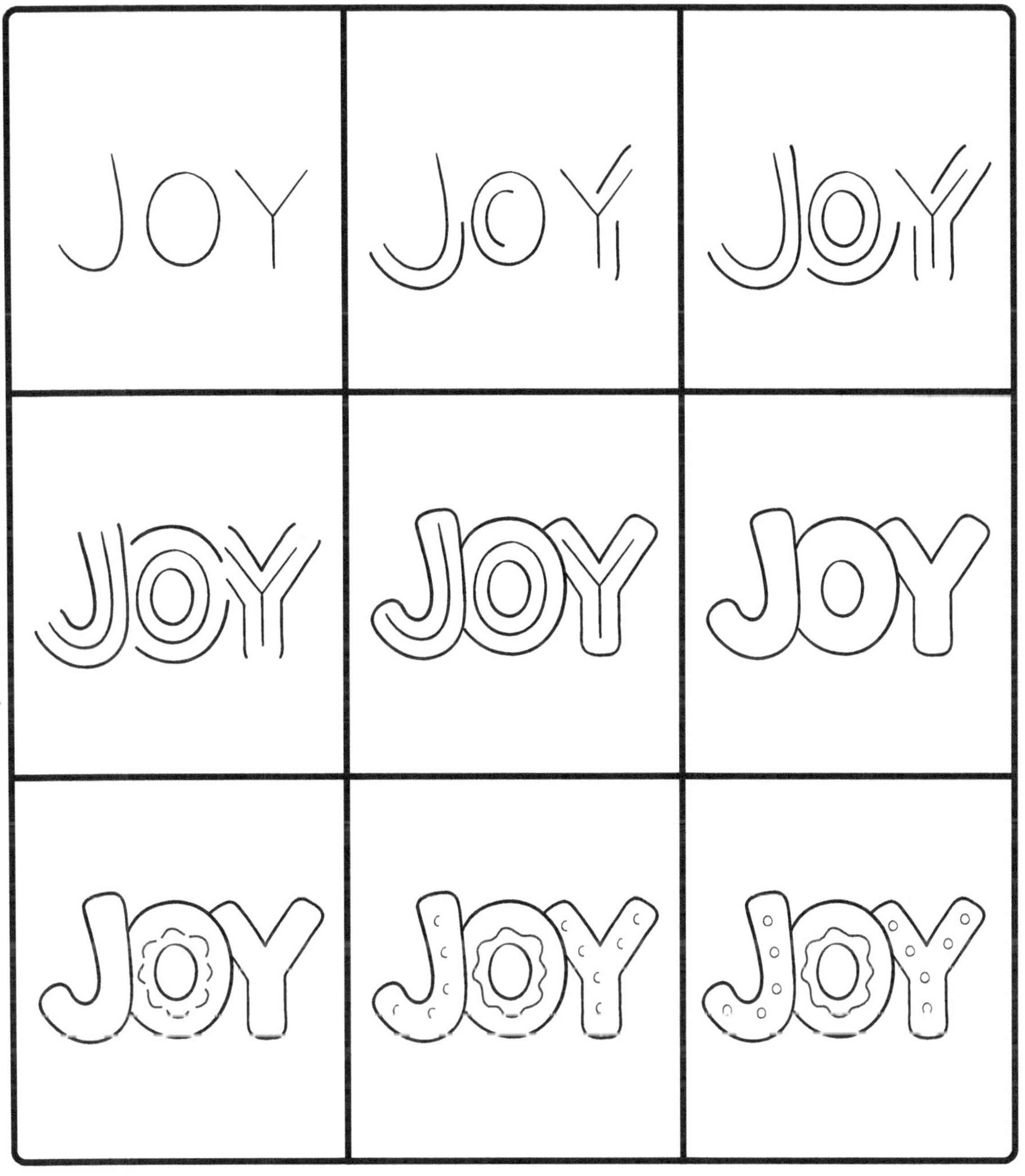

LOVEBUG

LIVES:
IN A COOKIE BOX.

LOVES MOST ABOUT CHRISTMAS:
THE SMILES ON FACES WHEN SHE IS
GIVEN AS A GIFT.

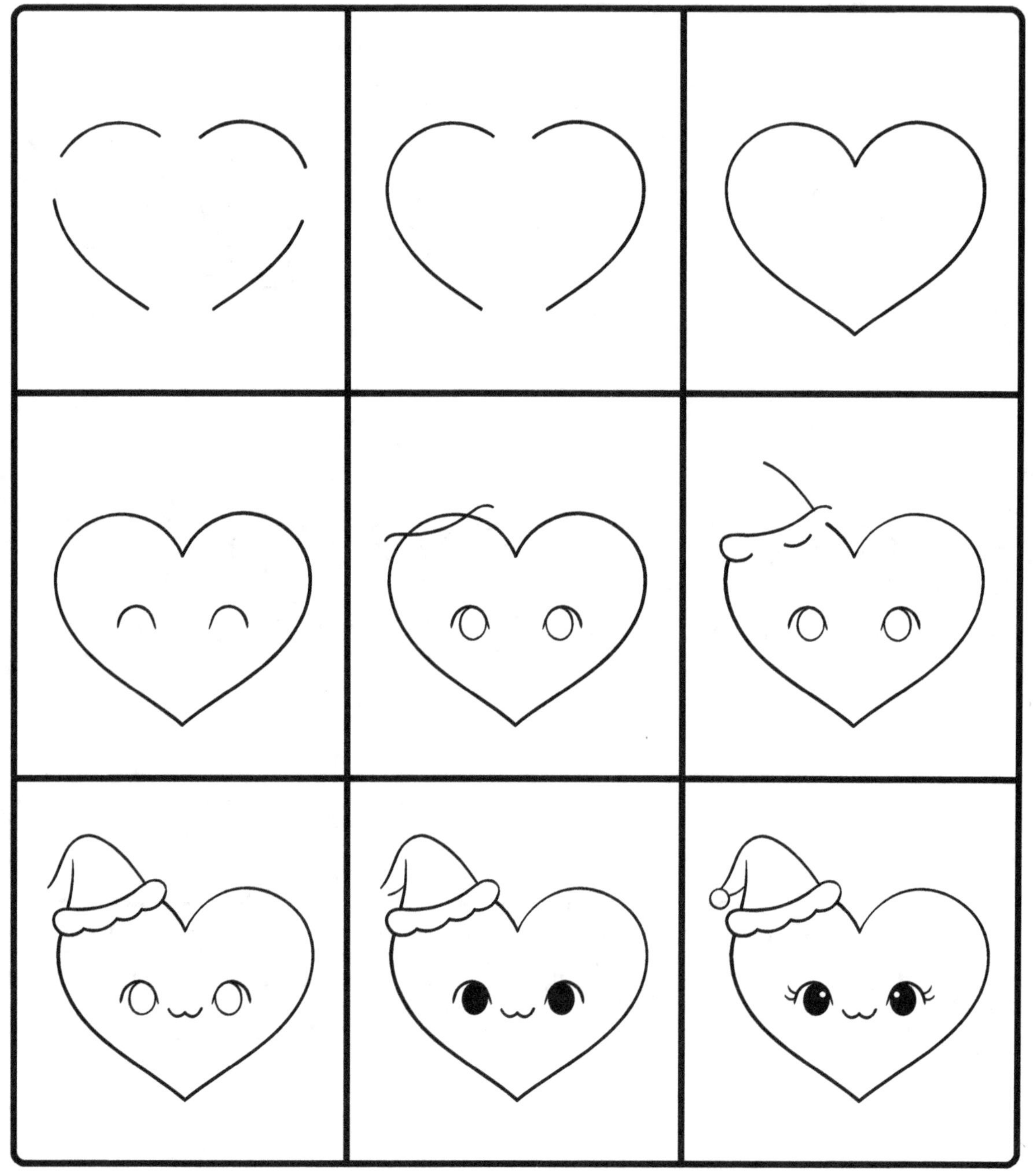

SANTA'S SIP

ON A LITTLE WOODEN TABLE NEXT TO THE FIREPLACE, READY FOR SANTA TO DRINK AFTER HE POPS OUT.

WARMING UP SANTA'S BELLY!

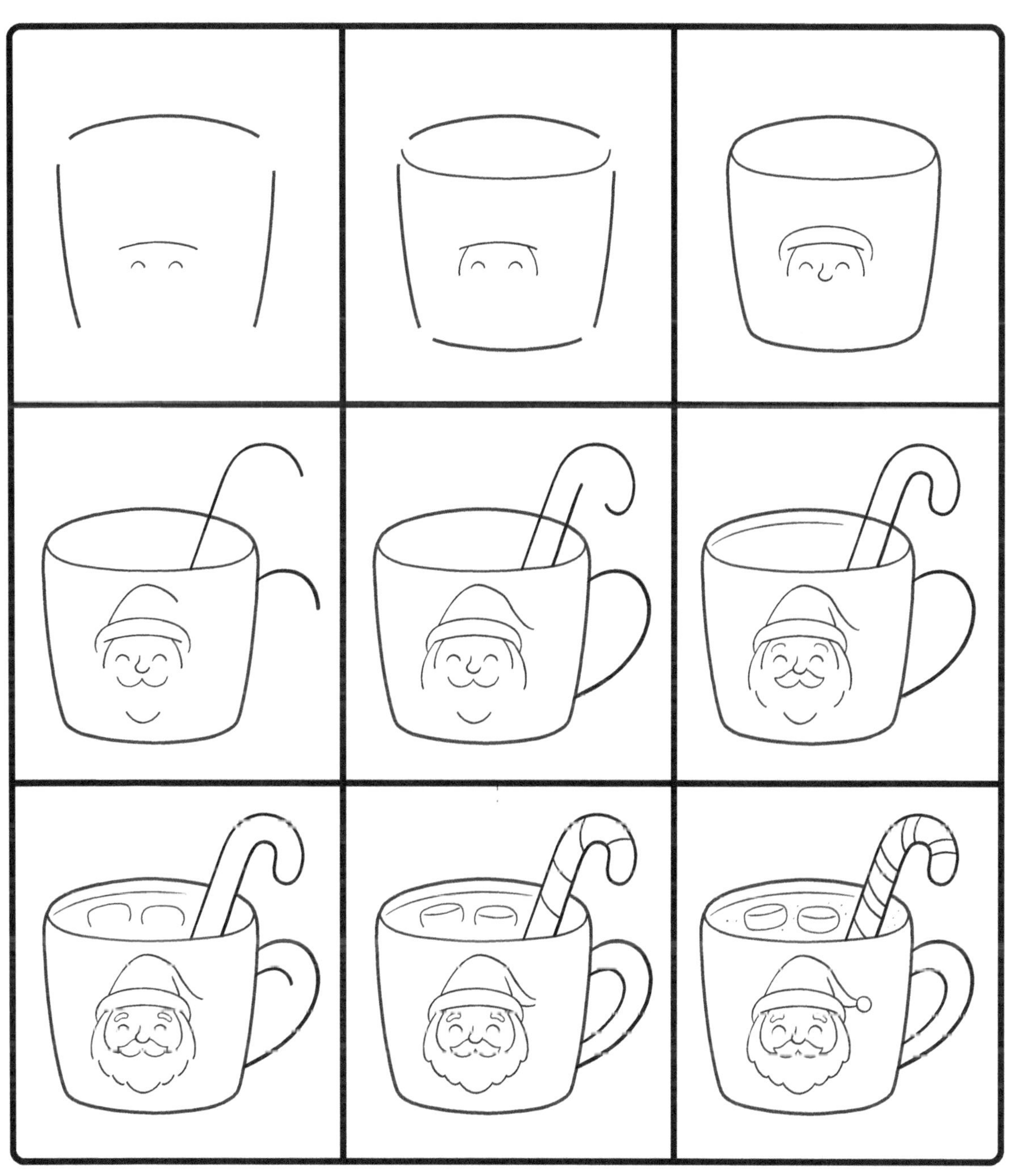

COZY KIT

LIVES:
IN A BASKET OF WOOL NEXT TO A LADY WHO LOVES TO KNIT CHRISTMAS SWEATERS.
LOVES MOST ABOUT CHRISTMAS:
SEEING THE WOOL SHE PLAYED WITH TURN INTO A SNUGGLY SWEATER.

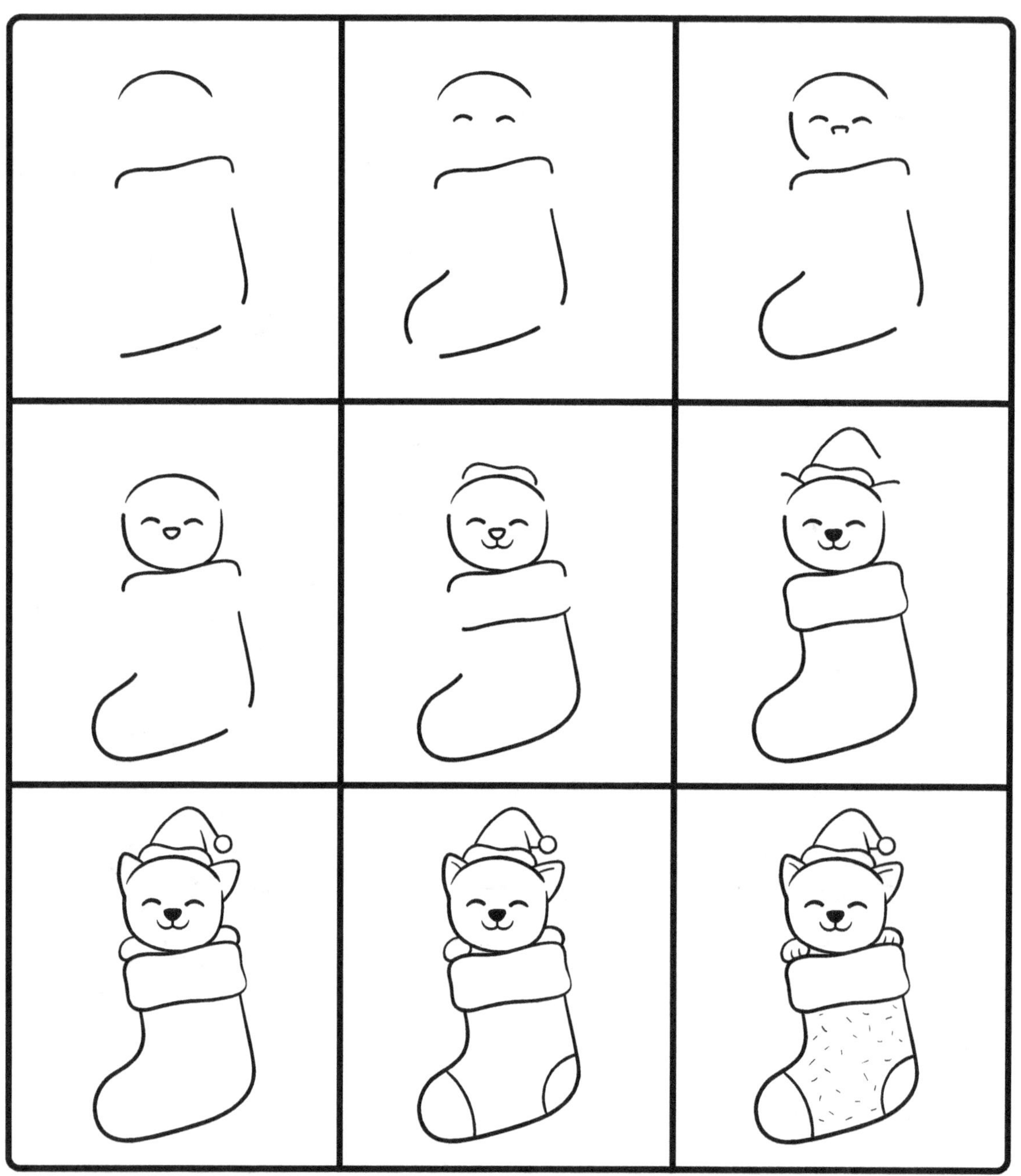

KITTY

LIVES:

IN A PRETTILY DECORATED BOX, DOTTED WITH HOLES, READY TO SURPRISE ON CHRISTMAS MORNING.

LOVES MOST ABOUT CHRISTMAS:

THE MOMENT THE LID IS PULLED OFF THE BOX AND THE HAPPY SMILES ON FACES.

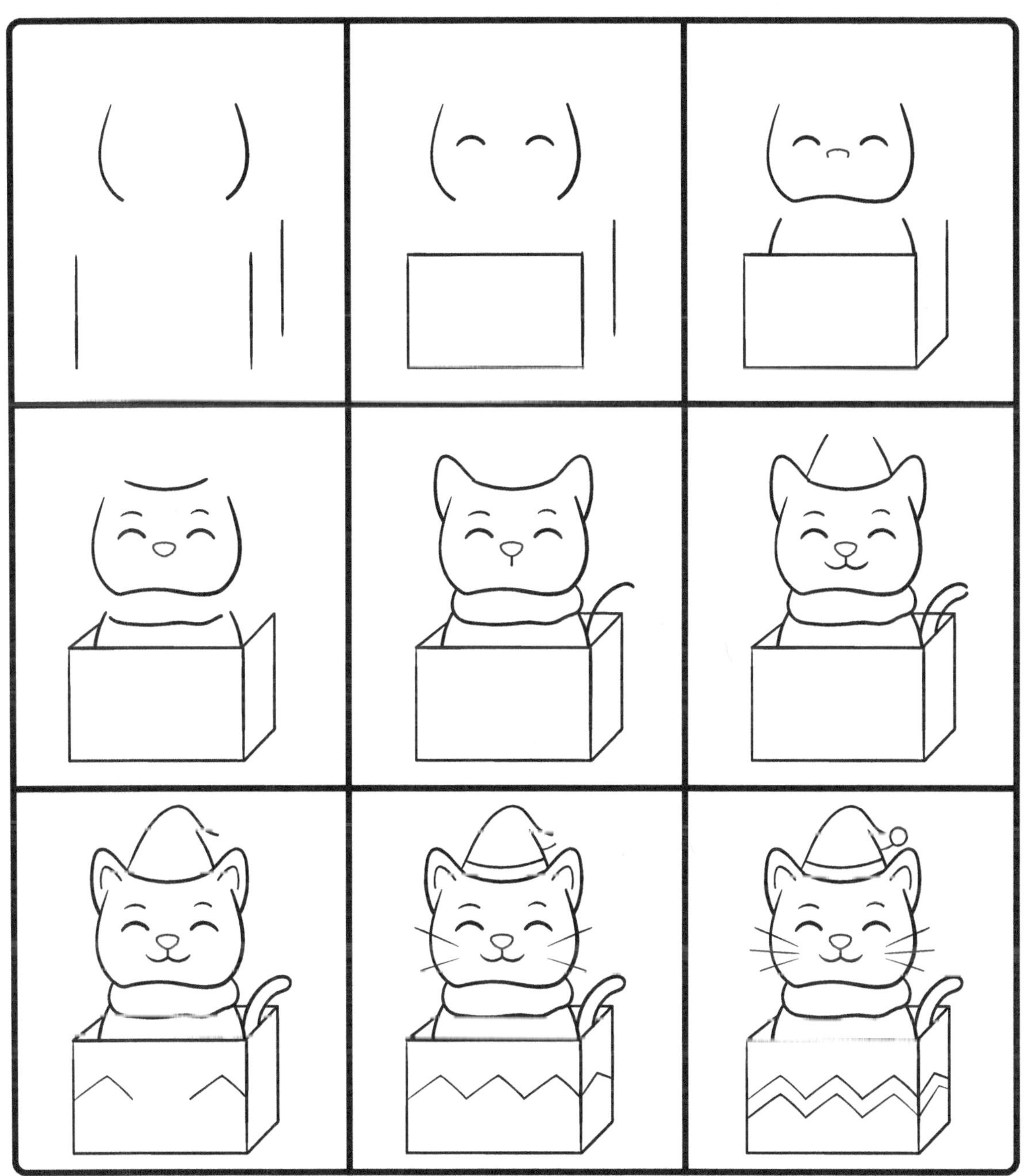

SNEAK

IN A COZY HOLE, UNDER A STAIRWELL.

THE REFLECTIONS OF THE CHRISTMAS
LIGHTS IN THE SNOW BELOW HIM.

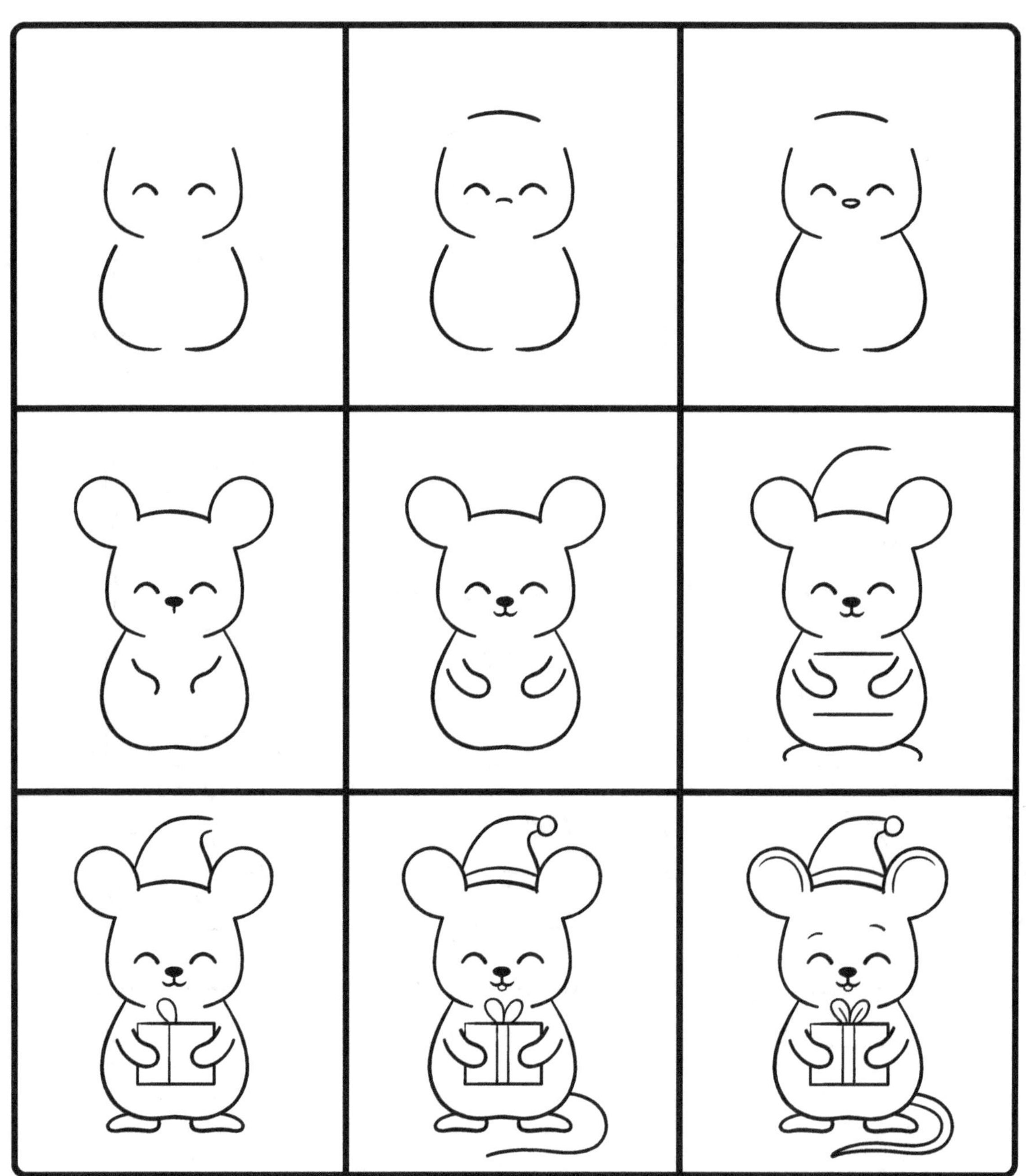

ALONG A BOULEVARD IN PARIS.

THE REFLECTIONS OF THE CHRISTMAS LIGHTS IN THE SNOW BELOW HIM.

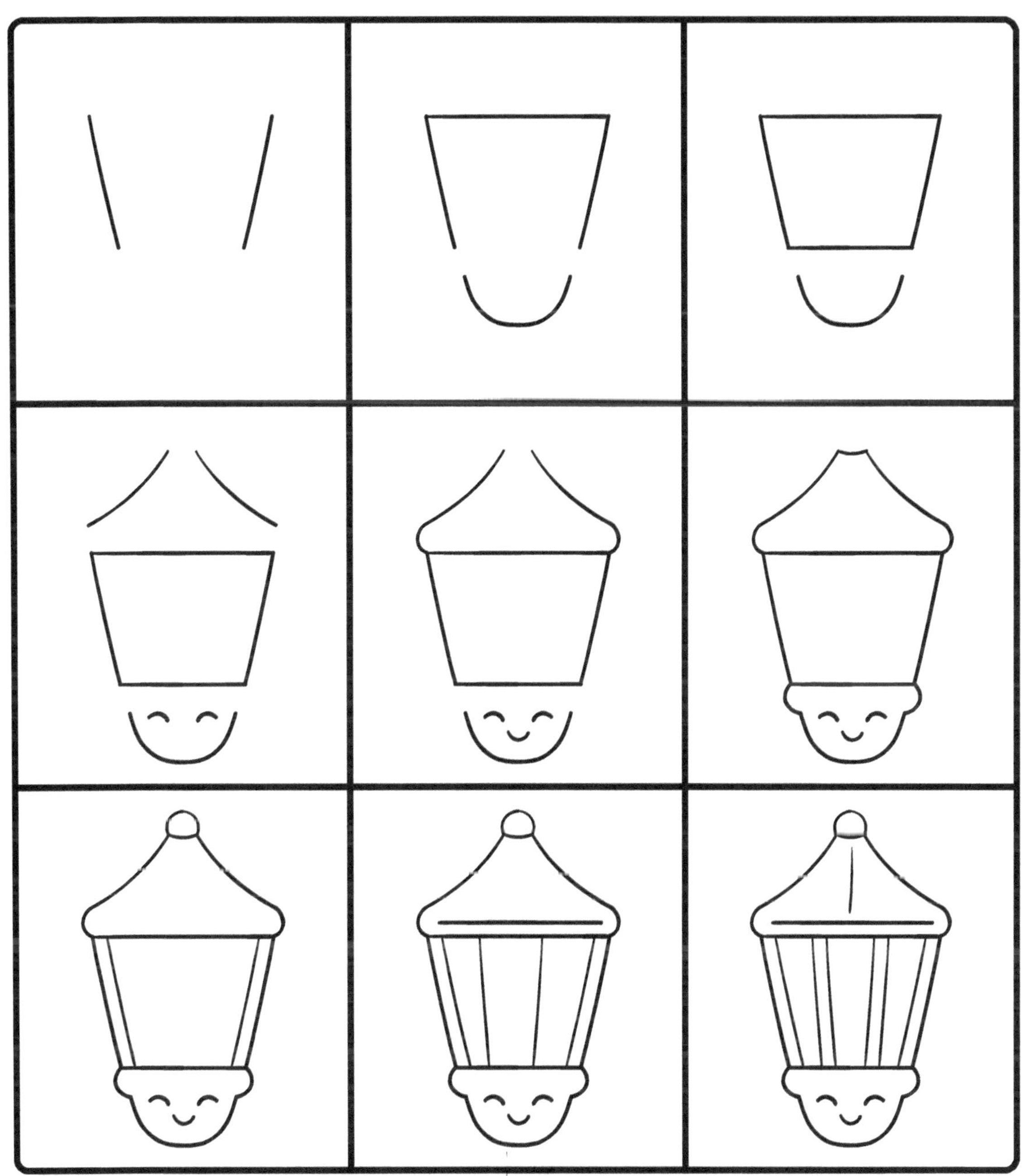

CAROL

LIVES:
IN THE EAVES OF A BUILDING ON THE EDGE OF A TOWN SQUARE.

LOVES MOST ABOUT CHRISTMAS:
JOINING IN WITH THE CAROLERS THAT SING ON CHRISTMAS EVE.

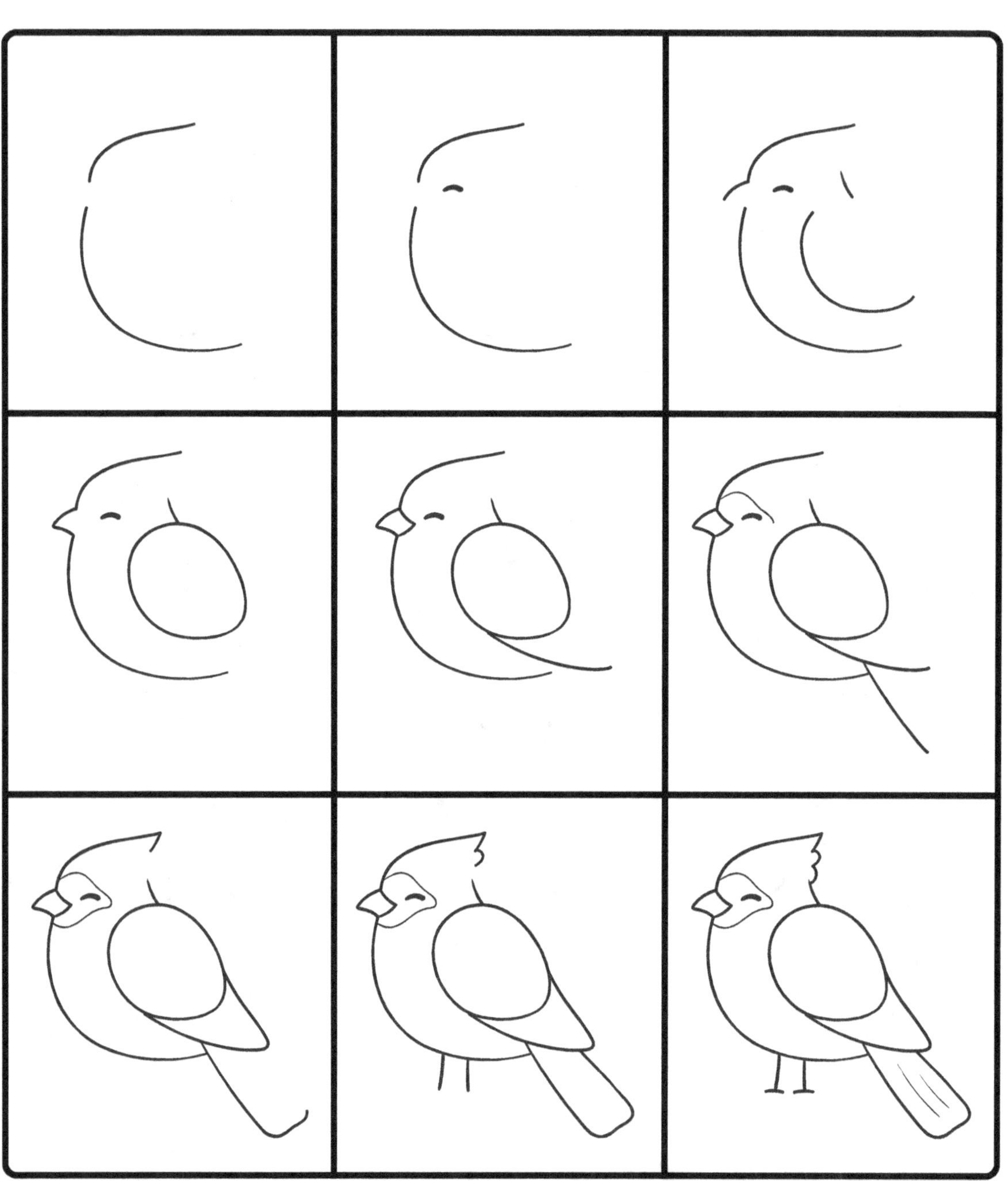

CHEERY

LIVES:
IN A LOG CABIN, DEEP IN A COLD, SNOW-DIPPED FOREST.

LOVES MOST ABOUT CHRISTMAS:
BEING DECORATED WITH STOCKINGS, CARDS, TINSEL, AND CHRISTMAS ORNAMENTS.

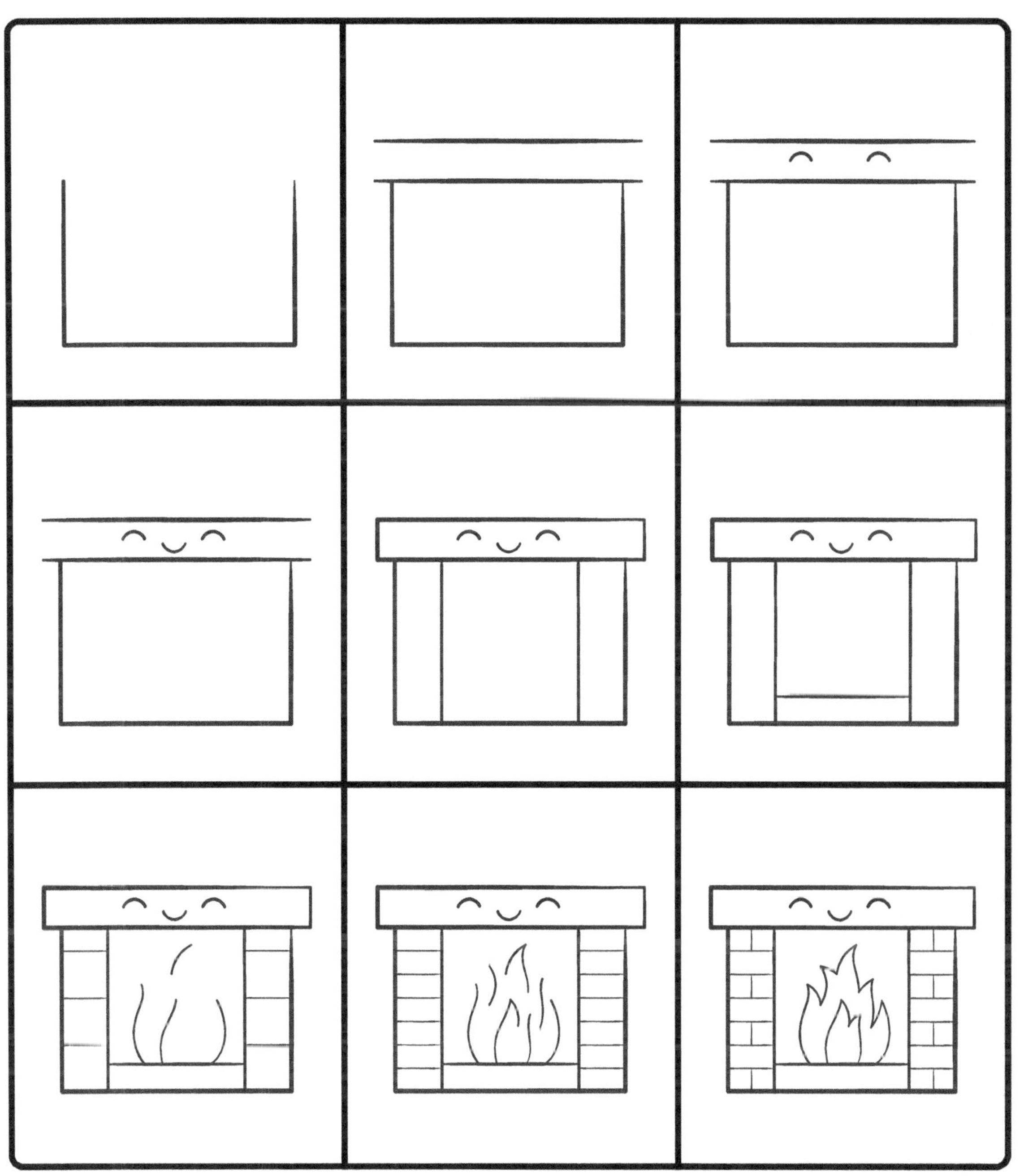

ANGIE

LIVES:
IN THE SKY, WAITING TO HELP WHEREVER SHE CAN.
LOVES MOST ABOUT CHRISTMAS:
MAKING EVERYONE'S WISHES COME TRUE.

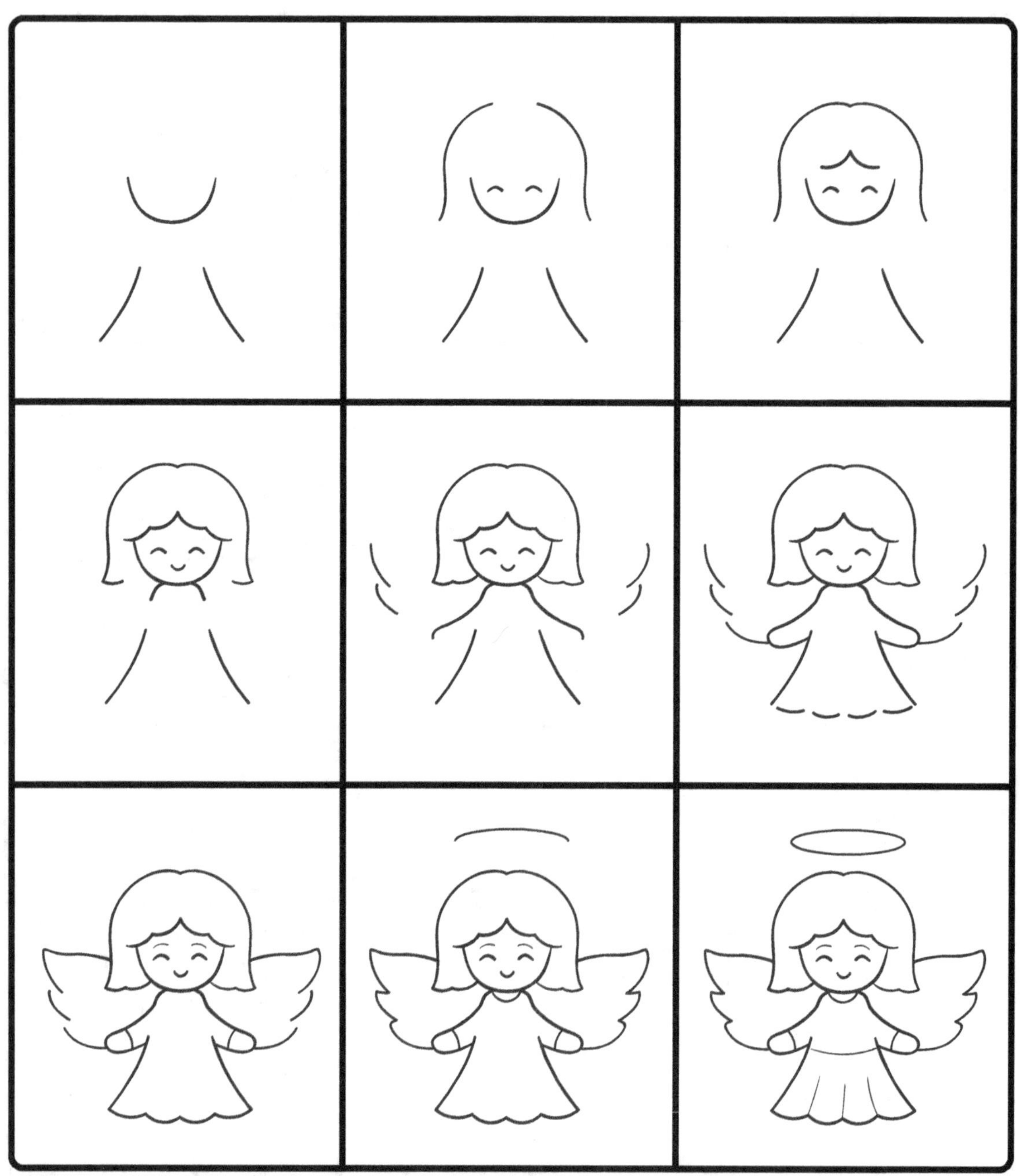

SWIFT

LIVES:
IN THE COLD WATERS OF CANADA.

LOVES MOST ABOUT CHRISTMAS:
WATCHING SANTA FLY ACROSS THE
NORTHERN LIGHTS.

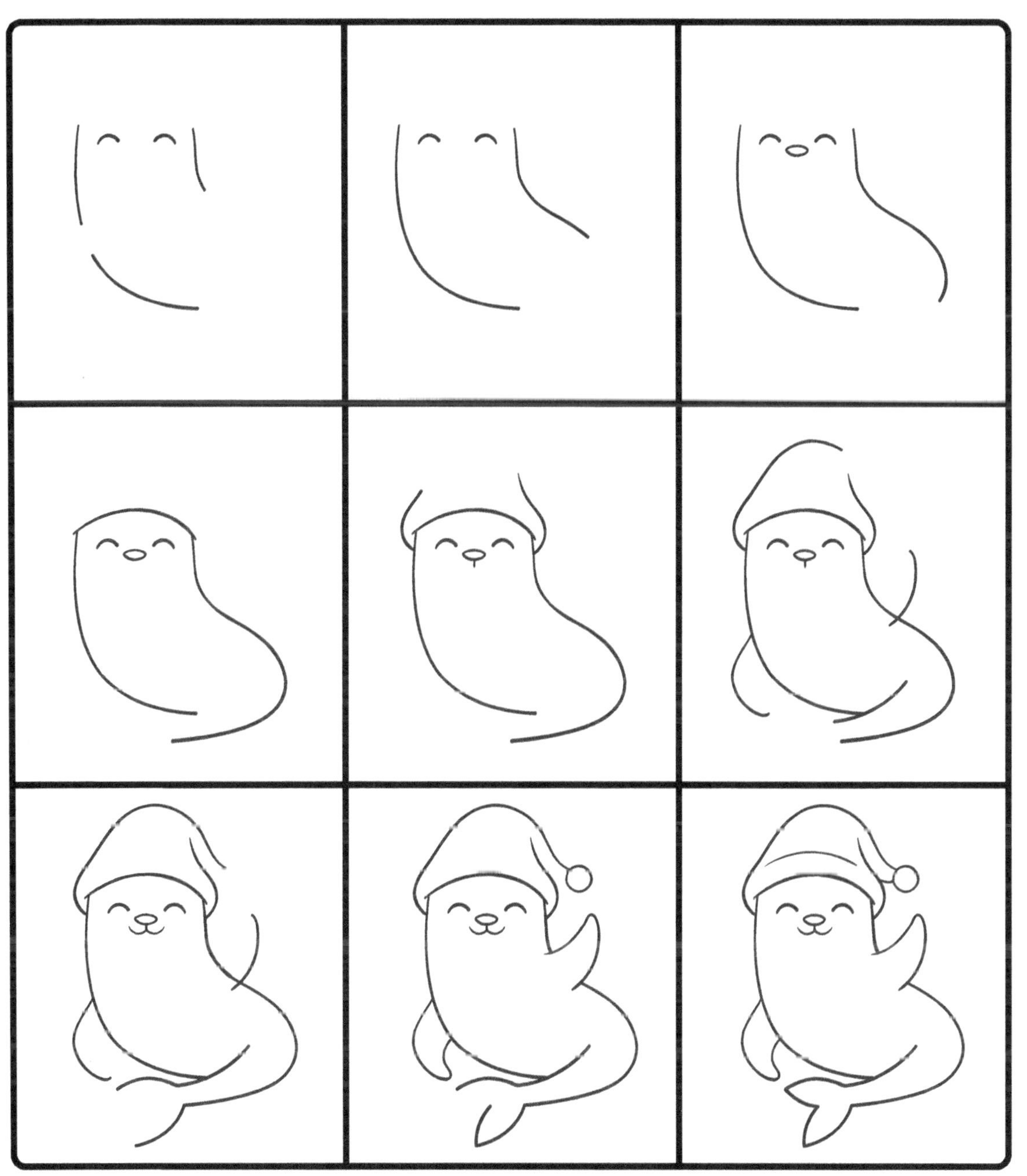

FLICKER

LIVES:
DRAPED ACROSS WINDOWS OF A
TOYSHOP IN THE CITY.

LOVES MOST ABOUT CHRISTMAS:
THE EXCITEMENT ON THE FACES OF KIDS
LOOKING IN THE WINDOW.

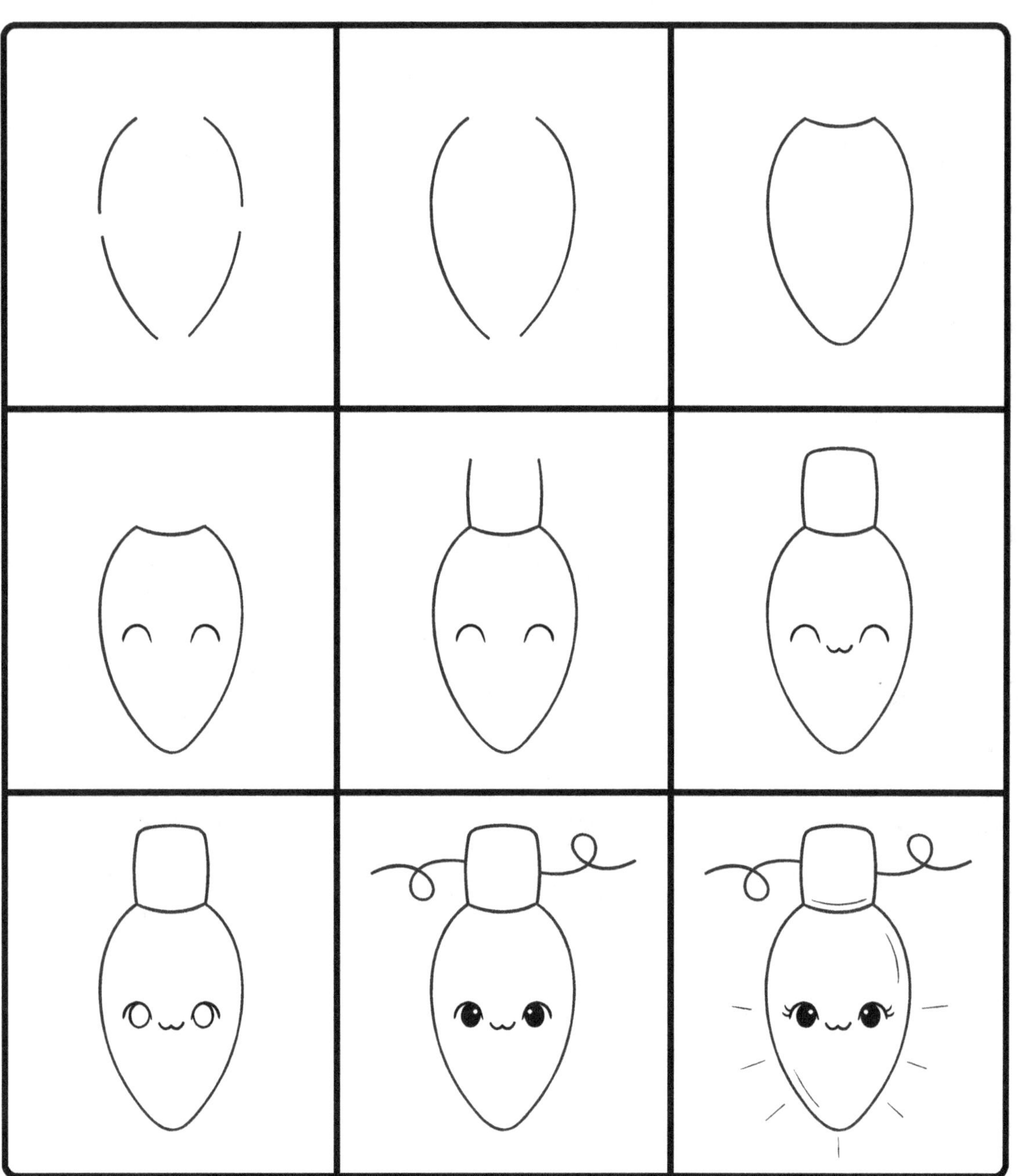

SMOKEY

LIVES:
ON TOP OF A TOWNHOUSE IN LONDON.

LOVES MOST ABOUT CHRISTMAS:
EACH YEAR WHEN SANTA CRAWLS INSIDE,
OF COURSE!

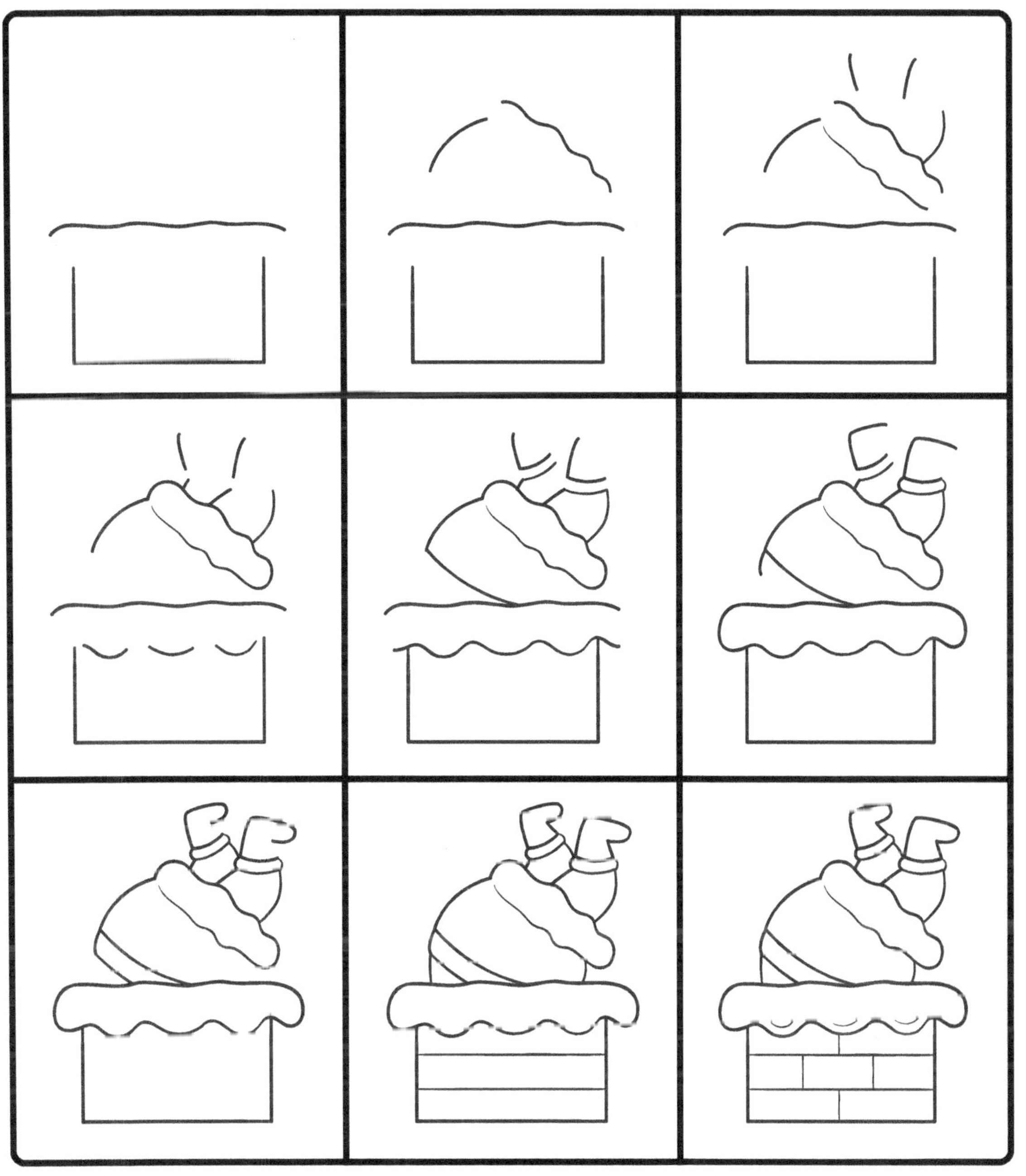

KRINGLE

HANGING FROM A TREE IN A SCHOOL CLASSROOM.

BEING PAINTED, THEN SPRINKLED WITH GLITTER AND BEADS.

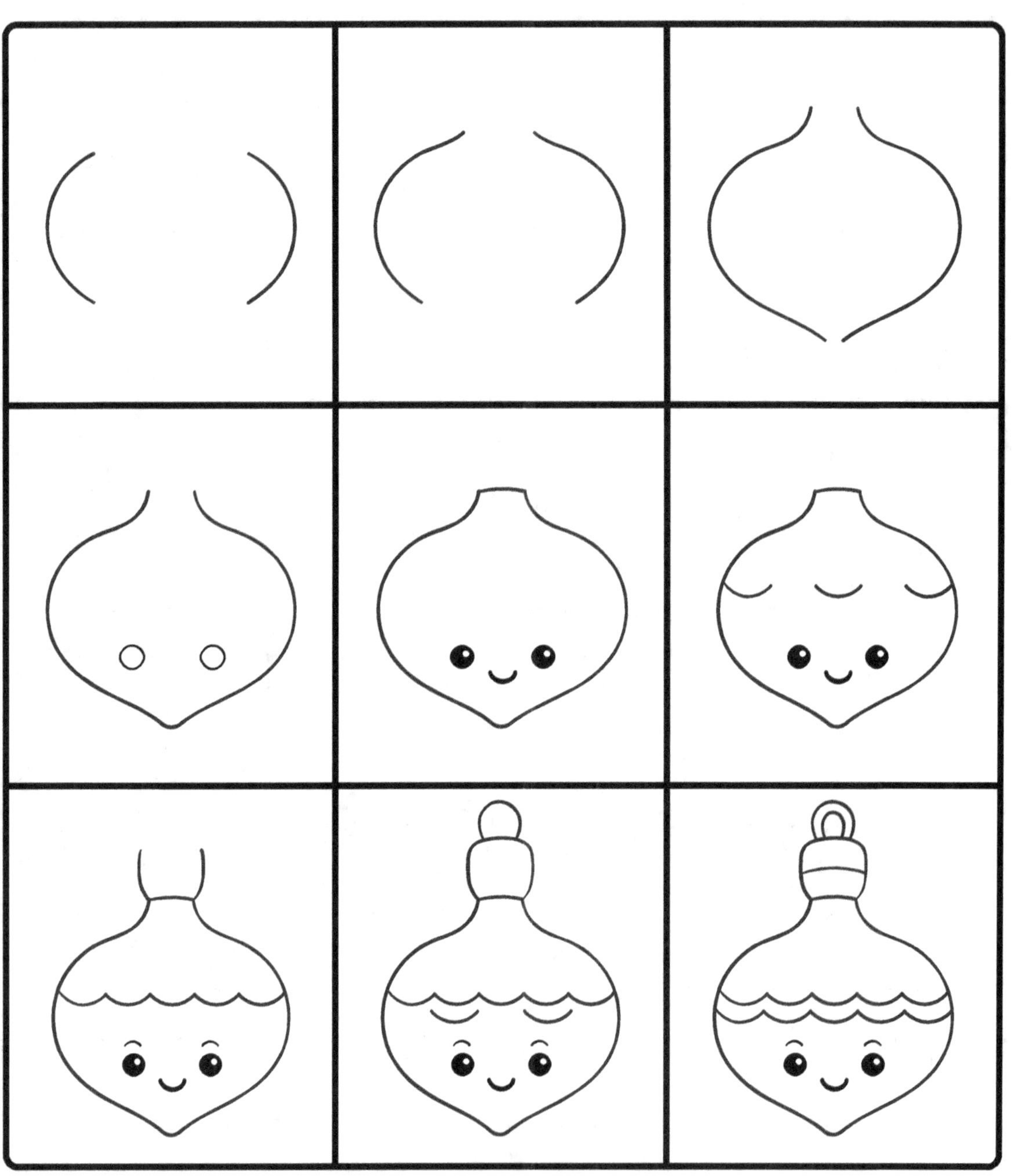

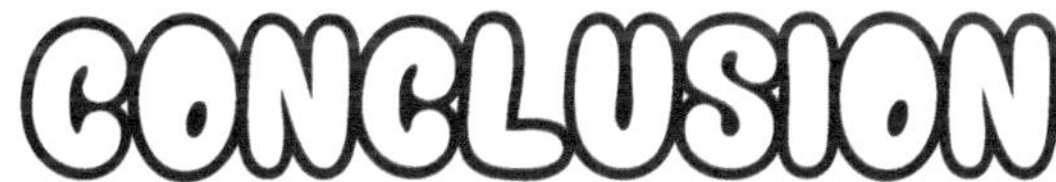 CONCLUSION

SO HOW DID YOU GO DRAWING THE CHRISTMAS OBJECTS AND CHARACTERS? WERE SOME TRICKIER THAN OTHERS? OR SOME MORE FUN TO DRAW?

NOW THAT YOU KNOW THE BASICS OF EACH DRAWING, YOU CAN NOW ADD YOUR OWN UNIQUE TOUCHES AND PERSONALITIES TO THEM!

IF YOU ENJOYED THE BOOK, PLEASE BE SURE TO LEAVE US A REVIEW ON AMAZON AS IT REALLY HELPS US GROW!